JASTA

and a third world war

KAMIL IDRIS

Design, typesetting and editing by UK Book Publishing

ISBN: 978-1-910223-89-5

www.ukbookpublishing.com

INTRODUCTION

If you are an American citizen and claim to be a victim of terrorism, US law (JASTA or 'Justice against sponsors of terrorism') will now allow you to sue any country which has a provable link to an attack. The Act was passed by both Houses of Congress, despite being vetoed by President Obama five days earlier, on September 28th, 2016.

Not surprisingly there has been a furious international reaction. While the law doesn't make direct mention of the 9/11 attacks, or the Kingdom of Saudi Arabia, the inference is clear. **The practical effect will be that US private citizens can file lawsuits against the Government of the Kingdom. In response Saudi Arabia and its allies have warned the US that allowing individuals to sue individual governments, thereby threatening their sovereignty immunity, could have very serious repercussions**.

There is also significant disquiet in US legal circles, which have been quick to point out that reciprocal laws from other countries could enact their own, similar laws, thereby posing a threat to US interests worldwide, adding to international tensions.

It is not difficult to see that if this legislation is acted on, or is not repealed, then many countries, including the US, could take up defensive stances to protect their immunity from prosecution. Curtis Bradley, a law professor at Duke University in North Carolina, explains: "It doesn't require that the foreign country did anything in the United States, it's not limited to just nations known to normally be associated with terrorism. Potentially any nation could be sued."

I believe that one of the ironies or side effects of the law would be that current counter terrorism partnerships would be undermined. Imagine if the US, for example, was cooperating closely with a certain country on key security issues and then suddenly allowed a series of lawsuits to be filed against it!

All of this is worrying enough, but if you add other factors into the international scene then ominous historical parallels begin to loom. At the risk of being accused of unnecessary alarmism, I will argue in this book that we are now as close as we have been since the Cuban missile crisis of 1962 to either a rapid escalation in global conflicts or even, a doomsday vision, a third world war, and, for a certain generation, the nuclear horrors of Nagasaki and Hiroshima are part of its collective nightmare. The parallels I have just mentioned also refer to the periods of political instability that led to the outbreak of two world wars. If we learn from history that we learn nothing from history then we are facing a bleak and disturbing future. However, if we can defuse these alarming developments with goodwill, common sense and an informed historical perspective we can breathe again and calm the waters of global discontent.

In the book I will make no concessions in favouring one country or the other. Any criticisms of governments I make will be expressed honestly and openly and I can say now that any fault I find will not be camouflaged in diplomatic niceties. It is my profound belief that if all countries can be rational and accepting of their mistakes then a solution can be found. To help find that solution I propose to outline as clearly as possible the roots of the current problem by an analysis of the past one hundred and fifty years. In fact I will go to the Mediterranean world to revisit the wisdom of ancient Rome.

It is a strange thing but even two thousand years ago precisely the same problems presented themselves and if the Romans could find a way out so can we.

Chapter One

IMPACT OF THE JASTA ACT ON FOREIGN RELATIONS

In the later chapters I examine the perils of extreme nationalism and the failure of the democracies to recognise the factors that led up to international conflicts, namely, in the twentieth century, the two world wars. Complacency, diplomatic inaction and a failure to learn from experience and history were the prime factors and I feel that there is an ominous similarity in the twenty first century to the twentieth. It is my intention to bring these factors into the light of day and by so doing highlighting the dangers of once again repeating historic and avoidable mistakes.

It is true that the JASTA Act could possibly discourage acts of international terrorism within the US but I think this is unlikely, given the fanatical motivation of terrorists who anyway have complete contempt for international law or boundaries. At this point I think it is important to express my profound sympathy for the victims and relatives of the 9/11 attack – an unprecedented crime in the modern history of mankind – and my complete condemnation of the terrorists and groups involved. My chief concern, however, is that JASTA will seriously affect the carefully established and sometimes precarious goodwill and understanding between the U.S. and other nations by attempting to undermine their legitimate sovereignty.

As previously stated, the area of immediate concern is JASTA. In my opinion this Act, passed by the US Congress, threatens the sovereignty of foreign nations and could force them into isolation, nationalism and a sense of grievance, destabilising the international scene and possibly forcing those nations into sudden and ill thought out alliances for protection. Section 3 of the Act actually amends the Federal Judicial Code, ensuring the reduction of the immunity of a foreign state from the jurisdiction of the American courts. This means that the federal courts have jurisdiction over a civil claim against a foreign state for death or physical injury to a property or a person that happened within the US due to an attack or an act of international terrorism committed by an agent, employee, or an official of a foreign country.

Under JASTA, therefore, a citizen of the US can launch a lawsuit against a foreign state for death, physical injury or damage caused by an act of international terrorism by a designated terrorist organisation. The citizen can then be compensated because section 4 of the Act gives the Federal Courts the power to impose civil liability on an individual who committed or supported an act of international terrorism authorised, planned or committed by a terrorist organisation. The Act is applicable to all civil claims of injury after or on September 11th, 2001 (Congress 2016, pars 1-5).

CRITICISM OF THE ACT

A number of international figures have already criticised the Act. The head of the Saudi-dominated Gulf Cooperation Council (GCC) voiced his worries about it two days after the House of Representatives passed it. And President Obama lobbied against it, arguing that it could have a detrimental effect on international relationships. He also pointed out that the Act violates the principle of Sovereign immunity (Staff 2016, pars.1,11).

5

VIOLATION OF THE SOVEREIGNTY
OF A FOREIGN STATE

Sovereignty is difficult to define clearly (Bartelson 2006, p.474). However, the term is commonly used to refer to the supreme authority and agency in a constitutionally autonomous, indivisible, and territorially exclusive political unit. JASTA threatens this supreme authority. The reaction of Saudi Arabia to the passing of the Act by the US Congress exposes this. Plaintiffs filing cases against foreign states will use legal systems of the US to prove their claims against foreign states. Tensions between the affected nations and the US will thus probably increase. This will happen especially if the foreign power is forced to reveal any relevant evidence in its possession (Berger, Sun, Spalding, 2016. p.4).

PRINCIPLES OF INTERNATIONAL LAW

A new law in the field of international law was introduced during the Berlin conference of 1885. The General Act justified the expansion of Europeans into Africa. It reasoned that primitive and uncivilised areas of the continent would benefit from the advantages that developed nations could promote. Even though the Act led to widespread colonisation, it was seen as beneficial by the Europeans to all concerned and that it was almost a duty for them to do so. By legalising this expansion, the Act justified the setting up of territorial boundaries and sovereignty. New international borders ensured that these initiatives gained recognition and authority, thus determining that sovereignty of foreign states has been respected and accepted ever since.

The consequent expansion of human rights led to discussions concerning relative sovereign immunity and also to debates about why states are not under the jurisdictions of courts within the territory of another nation.

This latter point was clarified during the "Pinochet" case in Europe and the "Prinz v. Federal Republic of Germany" in the US (Ex Parte Pinochet 1999, p.1; Prinz v. Federal Republic of Germany 1994, p.1). The idealists or supporters of human rights argued that sovereign immunity should be denied as a fundamental denial of human rights and for international crimes such as terrorism. On the other hand the realists, or the supporters of sovereign immunity, argued that countries are under an obligation to promote and uphold it to ensure the maintenance of peaceful and harmonious relationships between states.

The differences between the two sides have been tested in several court cases. Some of these cases include the "Arrest Warrant" case in the International Court of Justice (ICJ) and the "McElhinney and Al-Adsani" cases in the European Court of Human Rights (ECHR). The possibility of denying a foreign state immunity for reasons of war offences or offences against humanity was dealt with in the "Arrest Warrant"case (Arrest Warrant of 11 April 2000). In both cases the courts decided in favour of the realists; in other words they upheld the law (Al-Adsani v. UK 2001, p.24).

In the "Germany v. Italy, Greece intervening case", the ICJ concluded on February 3, 2012 that Italy had violated the sovereign immunity of Germany. According to the Court, sovereign immunity or State immunity should always be upheld in accordance with international customary law. Furthermore, the Court also argued that the rule should be upheld even if it is not unlawful (Jurisdictional Immunities of the State 2012, p.1).

Based on the conclusions of these cases JASTA has no standing in international law.

If certain States do not subscribe to a treaty's obligations they should nevertheless ensure that they do not trespass beyond the boundaries created by other doctrines of international law. For instance a State is required to avoid interfering in matters within another country. Furthermore it should recognise the sovereign equality of other States, including their political and territorial integrity ("Beckman and Butte", 2016, p.10).

THE FOREIGN SOVEREIGN IMMUNITIES ACT

Early in US history, The Supreme Court issued a ruling that made it possible to deny a foreign state sovereign immunity. In the "Schooner Exchange v. McFadden", the Court ruled that sovereign immunity is not a constitutional requirement but a matter of comity and grace. This stance was underwritten in the case of the decision of the Court in "Austria v. Altman" (Austria v. Altman 2004, p. 677). The same outcome was further supported in the "Samantar v. Yousuf" case (Samantar v. Youseuf 2010, p.1). The Court referenced the US Foreign Sovereign Immunities Act (FSIA) and **concluded that the Act did not apply to individuals**. The Court then made its decision based on Federal Common Law (Damrosh 2011, p.1187). Decisions touching on countries blamed by the US for supporting and promoting wrongful acts and acts of international terrorism have been under the jurisdiction of the US due to the FSIA. Examples of these cases involved the "Bennett, Acosta, Greenbaum and Heiser" creditors against the Republic of Iran.

The cases were held in different courts in the US and were based on a number of terrorist attacks that had happened between 1990 and 2002. The Bennett creditors claimed 13 million US dollars in damages from Iran for the bombing of a cafeteria at the Hebrew University in Jerusalem in 2002. Iran owed the Greenbaum creditors 20 million dollars for the bombing of a Jerusalem restaurant in 2001. The Acosta creditors were owed 590 million dollars by Iran after bombings in Saudi Arabia back in 1996. The US Congress enacted two statutes that would allow the US to have the right to take the assets of Iran and keep them in the US in the form of attachment. It formed the Terrorism Risk Insurance Act (TRIA) and USC.

The creditors also wanted to acquire 17.6 million dollars in blocked assets which were held by Visa and Franklin, but belonging to Bank Melli, the national bank of Iran. When Visa and Franklin went to court to prevent this move, they were asked to deposit the money at the Court's registry. Bank Melli sought to prevent this but was denied the chance by the District Court (Bennett v. Islamic *Republic of Iran 2015, p.2)*.

Even though FSIA seems to decide against the sovereign immunity of other countries, it is unlike JASTA. JASTA expands the non-commercial rule that is the exception to the FSIA. As states have become more involved in the world's commerce, they have agreed on a restrictive immunity that allows them to retain their sovereign immunity, being sued only for commercial dealings which are viewed to violate international law. Because of this, the legal case against the Bank of Iran did not raise tensions between the governments of Iran and the US

Section 1604 of the FSIA points out that foreign states are immune from jurisdiction of US courts. However, section 1605 gives exceptions to immunity to the sovereignty of a foreign nation. These exceptions include: when a foreign state relinquishes immunity; the claim involves a commercial activity linked to the US; or a claim of injury due to an act of terrorism supported by a foreign state. Even allowing for these exceptions, FSIA limits people's ability to sue a foreign state. **According to FSIA, for instance, a foreign**

state cannot be forced to pay for damages (Berger and Sun, 2016, p.2).

JASTA amends FSIA. Section 1605B of the Act allows the courts of the US to hear any case involving a foreign state. In this instance it violates the immunity of foreign nations. The relationship between one country and another is harmed when one of them denies the legitimacy of the other's sovereign immunity. The impasse can lead to serious tensions between the two nations and possibly to an international dispute (Negri 2014, p.125). This is clearly illustrated in the case of the German-Italian dispute. In its legal question, Germany requested to know whether Italy had violated the customary rule on immunity by suing Germany for its violation of international humanitarian law during the Second World War. It also wanted to know whether Italy did the same by constraining Germany's state property or by recognising a Greek judgement that demanded payments from Germany for the massacre of civilians in Distomo village in Greece during the same war (Finke 2011, p.854-855).

While Germany sought the help of the ICJ, other nations in the same situation may not seek the help of a court. They may decide to attack the other only for the purpose of protecting their sovereignty. Going back in history, this is precisely the situation that occurred in 1914 when Serbia refused to bring to justice the assassins involved in the death of Archduke Ferdinand of Austria-Hungary and his wife. Serbia demanded that the rules of sovereignty should apply and the stance was an indication that it did not want to be controlled by its powerful neighbour. It was a clear case of nationalism standing firm against outside pressure. This, of course, triggered the steps that eventually led to World War One. **The legal demands of Austria-Hungary led directly to the rise of Serbian Nationalism.**

A hundred years later the same situations occur. In 2010, after the deposing of President Kurmanek Bakiev of Kyrgystan, the Uzbeks, who formed the second largest community after that of the Kyrgyz, were rumoured to have burned the state flag and some of the Kyrgyz's properties. This enraged the Kyrygz who felt that their majority status and rights were under threat. This fear was intensified when the new Government called for greater involvement of Uzbeks in civil life. Understandably the Kyrygz assumed that their sovereignty as the largest community in the country was being violated. They decided to fight back. On the night of June 10th, 2010 the two ethnic groups clashed in a street fight and a large number of Uzbeks were killed. In addition some of their property was also destroyed.

The Kyrgyzstan Inquiry Commission(KIC) investigated the causes of the conflict and ruled that it was the Uzbeks who were to blame, but then recommended that the Government should fight ethnic exclusivity and extreme nationalism and should allow the Uzbek language to have special status in the country (Kyrgyzstan Inquiry Commission 2011, p.14). The Government was shocked by this decision and the amount of attention given to the Uzbeks.

It is my view that JASTA could be instrumental in increasing the likelihood of similar situations arising, such as the one of the Uzbeks in Kyrgyzstan. JASTA can undermine the sense of sovereignty of a nation, as it allows for the violation of that sovereignty. One of its most disturbing sections is for the allowance of a leader of a foreign state to come under the jurisdiction of a US federal court This could have catastrophic consequences as it will only intensify the outraged opinion of an accused state which will, in all likelihood, rally to the defence of their leader and lead to an escalation of national pride and the reclamation of their sovereignty. It could also instigate a process of events that, as in 1914, could lead to a third world war.

11

THE LEAGUE OF ARAB STATES

The negative reaction to JASTA has already been made clear in a number of states. The League of Arab States (LAS) has shown outright disapproval of the Act (Sharjah24 2016, par.1). According to the League, the Act lacks a political and legal base as it infringes on the sovereignty of other countries. This is a serious criticism as the League consists of twenty two countries from the Middle East and Africa.

The LAS was formed in 1945 and promotes the idea of Pan-Arabism and Arab nationalism. The member states aim to coordinate policies so that they can develop their economies and safeguard their sovereignty and independence (Arab League Online 2014, pars.3-4). For this reason, all of these states will reject the introduction and application of JASTA, leading to an unwelcome increase in tension between them and the US. Saudi Arabia in particular will reject the Act because it is one of the members of the League that is blamed for the September 11, 2001 attack.

A lawsuit has already been filed against Saudi Arabia by an American called Stephanie DeSimone, only two days after the Act was made law. She claims that Saudi Arabia is partly to blame for the death of her husband during the above mentioned attacks. According to her, Saudi Arabia funded Al Qaeda and probably knew about its plans to attack the US (Clary 2016, par. 2-3). Saudi Arabia has always maintained good relationships with the US, acknowledging its interest in Saudi oil. In fact Saudi Arabia led the development of the Organisation of Petroleum Exporting Countries (OPEC) in order to help and enable countries to gain control over their own resources. Iran had formerly used its oil resources as an anti-Western weapon but didn't achieve its objective because of the huge amounts of oil already in the open market and it was then that Saudi Arabia saw the need for an organisation of oil producing countries. Together with Iraq, Saudi Arabia now produces a third of the total capacity of the OPEC countries.

This was a formidable alliance of countries and its impact was felt in 1973 when OPEC used oil as a weapon against countries supporting the Camp David Accords and Israel (Baalke 2014, p.7). Even though Saudi Arabia was affected negatively, its part in the tactic was significant.

In my opinion it is now in a similar position of influence to fight the introduction of JASTA. However this is problematic because the ACT places responsibilities of action against another country in the hands of courts and private litigants (The White House 2106, par.5) and not in the hands of a government.

This effectively means that the Federal Government of the US cannot intervene on its behalf or negotiate with other countries on legal matters affecting their relationship. It is highly likely, therefore, that friction between the two countries will inevitably follow.

COUNTERACCUSATION

JASTA is likely to lead to other countries adopting similar acts which would lead to the US itself facing lawsuits from all over the world. This was why President Obama himself was so critical of JASTA during the last few months of his administration. According to him, the US had tried to compensate foreign victims of US action through voluntary compensation programs but he now fears that states that are threatened by JASTA may allow their own citizens to make reciprocal claims against the US. This is a strong possibility because an Iraqi lobbyist group has already used

JASTA to argue that Iraqis ought to be compensated by the US for the damages incurred during its invasion of Iraq in 2003 (Berger and Sun 2016, p.4).

President Obama's stance is understandable, given the fact that the US has also been accused of committing alleged international crimes, yet the Act makes no recognition of them. Following the 9/11 attacks the US has been blamed for a number of atrocities associated with anti-terrorism programs. It decided to retaliate for the attacks by using all the weapons at its disposal, including diplomacy, economic sanctions, international cooperation, enhancement of physical security and military force (Perl 2006, 4).

The use of military force has inevitably brought civilian casualties and destruction of property wherever it has been applied. There were efforts to avoid these where possible but there have been reports that by June 2011 more than three thousand innocent people had been killed by US drones, yet the CIA admitted to only 125 of them (Zulaika 2014, p.71). This anomaly could have been a consequence of the difficulty in identifying terrorists as apart from civilians. Doubts about the guilt of prisoners in Guantanamo Bay have also been raised. Among the 779 men detained about 700 have been released (Zulaika 2014, p.171). It is obvious now that many of these prisoners were detained on dubious grounds.

The Bureau of Investigative Journalism in London noted that 2,972 to 4,520 people have been murdered using drones up to September 2012 in Pakistan. Among these were 177 children, while 545 to 1001 were innocent adult civilians (Llenza 2011, p. 47). Other Western organisations made counter claims that about 85% of those killed using drones were militants but Pakistan disputed this. According to "The News", a Pakistani daily newspaper, only 14 people among 701 who were the victims of drones in the period between 2006 and 2007 were militants (Zulaika 2014, p.171).

The US claims that it goes to extreme lengths to avoid civilian casualties but accidents do happen. When a US drone was used to kill Baitullah Mehsud, who was a leader of the Taliban in Pakistan, his seven bodyguards, his wife, a lieutenant, his uncle and his in-laws were killed instantly (Llenza 2011, p.47).

In a similar case a US drone dropped three missiles on a group of five men seated behind a local mosque in Kashmir on 29th August 2012 again killing them instantly. The Defence Ministry of Yemen claimed that three of the men were members of Al-Qaeda who were meeting their associates. However, the other two men were not members of any group. Salim Aji Jaber was a cleric who had been preaching against the violent methods that Al-Qaeda was using. The other man was Walid bin Ali Jaber, the cleric's cousin, who, at the time of his death, was a police officer. The three members of Al-Qaeda had asked to meet the cleric because of his anti Al-Qaeda sentiments. His cousin had accompanied him as a protective measure. The killing of these two innocents highlighted the dangers of using indiscriminate weapons and in fact is a violation of international humanitarian law (Human Rights Watch 2013, p.1).

It is for reasons similar to the ones just mentioned that, in engaging in accusations of violence against other countries, the US is laying itself open to counter accusations that could point to its own failings in complying with international law.

Even though the US is claiming the moral high ground, it is inevitable that international opinion will conclude that it is also accused of double standards.

There is also a complementary war of propaganda at play and many insurgent groups have utilised the failures of the US to their advantage. The Taliban, for example, has portrayed the US as some form of colonial power aiming to control and manipulate the Afghan Government. The presence of their soldiers helping with the maintenance of security in the country only underlines this suspicion (Taddeo 2010, p.287). As a consequence the image of the US among the civilians of Afghanistan and Pakistan is far from healthy and resentment at their influence is growing.

As a result of intensified US military operations the number of insurgents has grown from 1,500 to 30,000 in 2012 (Dreyfuss 2013, pl.).

In the 1990s a combination of Arab nationalism and religious fervour militated against favourable diplomatic relations with the US (Demirpolat 2009, p.87). **I believe the friction between the two countries could intensify if JASTA is fully implemented.** I think one of the things people in the West find difficult to understand is that Muslims from different countries feel themselves to be brothers, despite their allegiances to their country of origin. In other words religion can sometimes trump patriotism (Carlo 2016, pars.2-3). There is, therefore, a possibility that if a Muslim feels that his brother in one country is being unfairly treated, his instinct might be to bond with and support him, particularly if there is a suggestion that he is being singled out because of his religion. Insurgents have been quick to proclaim that this is the real motive behind the strategy of the US in encroaching into Muslim territory. This theory can have a twofold effect on the Muslim world though. On the one hand there is a feeling of unity and solidarity in the face of outside aggression, but on the other there is also scope for disunity because of complex differences between Muslims themselves. **On balance, however, I feel that the current misunderstandings of the US in addressing the concerns of Afghans and Pakistanis, and others, and their underestimating the effects of JASTA, will lead to a**

deterioration in relationships between the two sides.

If JASTA is fully implemented and not repealed, citizens of affected countries will interpret the Act as one sided and morally selective, simply because the US seems to be unaware of its own transgressions of International Law.

The consequence of this will be the withdrawing of goodwill, the possible cancelling of diplomatic relations and a growing move to nationalism, as country after country feels a common sense of injustice at the perceived injustice of the Act.

Chapter Two

A LESSON FROM HISTORY

I believe that in 2017 the world is entering a dangerous phase, exhibiting similar political and social trends that were prevalent just before the outbreak of the first and second world wars and it is my intention to alert as many right minded people as possible to the paths that might lead away from conflict and even a third, disastrous third world war.

To analyse and gain perspective I need to go back two thousand years to ancient Rome where similar parallels to today's global scenario were noted by a man called Marcus Tullius Cicero. He was one of the empire's greatest statesmen, and his insights into politics, morality and the law still ring true today. It was he in fact, among others, whom the American founders looked to when they drafted their Constitution in 1787. He lived at the time of the disintegration of the Roman republic, when the first emperors, the Caesars, were about to take control of the republic and became, effectively, dictators. Shakespeare captured it all in his play "Julius Caesar", particularly in the character of Brutus, the incorruptible defender of free speech, democracy and public morality. When asked if he would join the conspiracy to assassinate Julius Caesar, the man who threatened Rome with dictatorship, Brutus gave the unforgettable reply: "If it be anything towards the general good, set honour in one eye and death in the other and I will look on both indifferently." In other words he believed in the unshakable values of democracy and freedom and would fight a tyrant or dictator to the last drop of his blood, which he eventually did, falling on his own sword at the battle of Philippi in 42 BCE.

Cicero was a man of similar convictions and nobility of nature to Brutus. He was retired from politics and at the age of 64 calmly waited in his seaside villa north of Naples for Mark Antony's soldiers to execute him, after he had joined the conspiracy to assassinate Caesar.

I mention Cicero because it was his analysis of Rome's decline, its lack of belief in its republican constitution, the distancing of the political elite from its ordinary citizens and its breathtaking corruption, that typify much of what is currently happening in the world today.

He was able to make these judgements from a firm moral standpoint based on his belief in what he called "The natural law". This wasn't a manmade system of carefully thought out ethical standards, but an understanding that a divine providence was at work in the universe, and that mankind was able to tap into its key components of reason and eternal religious truths that help to form civil laws and shape society. Or, as he put it: "Man is a single species which has a share in divine reason and is bound together by a partnership in Justice."

This wasn't just a political recipe for Ancient Rome, it was for all time and all societies and it is worth remembering that the great democracies of the Anglo-Saxon world were based on precisely these principles. Even the UN's Declaration of Human Rights bows in gratitude to the writings of Cicero.

He saw very clearly that when Rome turned its back on its fundamental principles the result was social breakdown and a crisis of leadership. The symptoms that he highlighted, factionalism, corruption, selfish ambition, a polarising of opinion and social inequalities can be seen today, especially in the West, where respect for the traditions of republican or democratic standards have been under attack from liberal elites, secular values and politically correct denial of freedom of speech. One of the key dangers Cicero identified was the undermining of civic virtue and duty by ambitious men interested solely in power for its own sake. Instead of serving the state out of a sense of responsibility for the common good, it was a case of winning the election and then seeing what happens. There was absolutely no place for conviction politicians and the ruthlessly greedy money men would barge their way to the top.

As a great orator, Cicero was driven by an absolute conviction that if men were to govern, then their first priority was to govern themselves. He would have ridiculed the current view that what men do in their private lives doesn't matter so long as they are effective politicians. He believed in a private morality translating itself into the public sphere for the common good and he thus set a standard or template for leadership down through the centuries. Echoes of his rhetorical style can be heard in the magnificent speeches of two of the mightiest defenders of freedom, Abraham Lincoln, Nelson Mandela and Winston Churchill. Below is the text of the Gettysburg address, Lincoln's famous lines commemorating the dead of both sides in the US civil war in 1863. It lasted only two minutes and has gone down in history as one of the finest speeches of all time.

"Four score and seven years ago our fathers brought forth on this continent, a new nation, conceived in Liberty, and dedicated to the proposition that all men are created equal.

Now we are engaged in a great civil war, testing whether

that nation, or any nation so conceived and so dedicated, can long endure. We are met on a great battle-field of that war. We have come to dedicate a portion of that field, as a final resting place for those who here gave their lives that that nation might live. It is altogether fitting and proper that we should do this.

But, in a larger sense, we can not dedicate – we can not consecrate – we can not hallow – this ground. The brave men, living and dead, who struggled here, have consecrated it, far above our poor power to add or detract. The world will little note, nor long remember what we say here, but it can never forget what they did here. It is for us the living, rather, to be dedicated here to the unfinished work which they who fought here have thus far so nobly advanced. It is rather for us to be here dedicated to the great task remaining before us – that from these honored dead we take increased devotion to that cause for which they gave the last full measure of devotion – that we here highly resolve that these dead shall not have died in vain – that this nation, under God, shall have a new birth of freedom – and that government of the people, by the people, for the people, shall not perish from the earth."

It was Lincoln, and men like him, who believed that the best way to prevent men of ambition from seeking power was to ensure that a government's first priority was expressed in those final two lines.

Rome in Cicero's time was riven by corruption, violence and the naked ambition of those seeking power for its own sake, their values being polar opposites of the kind Lincoln was expressing. Cicero blamed this on the abandoning of universal moral laws and increased levels of materialism, and contempt for the values of civic and political life.

Chapter Three

EFFECTS OF A NUCLEAR WAR

If JASTA is fully implemented I am arguing that there could be a consequent retreat into a hardening form of nationalism as a protective measure. A further consequence could be a heightening of international tensions as new alliances are formed and old ones disappear. It is quite possible that in such a nervous and unstable world nuclear options could come into play as no longer unthinkable.

"Now I am become death, the destroyer of worlds." When US scientist J. Robert Oppenheimer witnessed the first nuclear bomb testing on July the 16th, 1945 he quoted from the Bhagavad Gita to express his horror at the scale of its power.

Four years later the future President Eisenhower warned that he didn't know how a third world war might start but he knew how one would be fought: "With rocks".

Seventy years later the world has developed weapons hundreds of times more powerful than the ones dropped on Nagasaki and Hiroshima and now has the capacity to destroy all forms of life.

At present there are five countries that have nuclear weapons and the ability to launch them across thousands of miles. They are: USA, Russia, UK, France and China. India, Pakistan, and North Korea have nuclear weapons and are developing missiles capable of reaching targets up to fifteen hundred miles away. Israel is an unknown quantity, neither denying nor confirming that it possesses them.

Thankfully, since the end of the Second World War, there has been a lengthy standoff between the USA and the former Soviet Union, now Russia. This arrangement used to be sub-titled "MAD" or "mutually agreed destruction". Even if there had been a pre-emptive sudden strike by one side, there would still have been enough firepower in the defending country to retaliate, almost guaranteeing total destruction, not just of their own countries but probably most of the globe as well.

What is of major concern is not so much the stockpiling and the potential for "overkill" but human error. When a US president assumes office one of his or her first duties is to attend a briefing session from the security services. He or she will be given a small card with the codes needed to talk to the Pentagon to confirm his or her identity in the event of a national security crisis. Just supposing he loses the card, as, allegedly, did Bill Clinton who lost his wallet with the card in, and as, allegedly, did Jimmy Carter when he sent a pair of trousers to the cleaners with the card inside a pocket – so Armageddon and the future of the world could be detonated by simple absent mindedness.

The picture is further complicated with a new US President assuming office.

True, Mr Trump has made softening overtures to Vladimir Putin and it looks like he is keen to defuse any simmering tensions lingering from the Obama presidency. At the moment, both the

US and Russia have signed an arms treaty, limiting their strategic arsenals of weapons, called New Start, which expires in 2021 and tens of billions of dollars could be saved if the treaty were to be extended. There would have to be concessions from both sides, however, and it would be likely that Putin would seek for a reduction, or even scrapping of, the US missile defence system in Europe. In my opinion this would send shivers down the spines of European leaders as protection would be withdrawn.

President Trump's briefing by the security services would also include mention of the nuclear capabilities of North Korea and, to a lesser extent, Iran, both of which are looked at in a later chapter.

My reason for raising the issue of these nuclear weapons is because, as I have already stated, I believe we are close to mirroring the conditions that eventually led up to the First World War. It is imperative that we learn and apply the lessons of history and we ignore the facts at our peril. For example, there was a consensus of opinion in 1914, that if there was going to be a war, it would be short, limited to border skirmishes or set piece encounters and fought in a traditional manner. The battles would be fought on carefully chosen sites with cavalry accompanying the infantry. What shocked the world was that the reality of twentieth century war was light years away from this assumption. It was brutal, fought with terrifying new weapons, including tanks, poison gas and aircraft, and, for the first time, mass destruction of civilian populations and cities. Very few people had foreseen this and the tragedy was that once it had started it was almost impossible for it to stop.

This is why the later chapters are going to make disturbing reading as I am going to examine what are considered to be the real effects of a third world war.

I think most people have some idea of the appalling power of a nuclear bomb. We have all seen pictures of Nagasaki and Hiroshima after the air strikes but when we hear that twenty first century bombs are hundreds of times more devastating the imagination shuts down. In short we are in almost the same situation as people were in 1914. We close our eyes and pretend that this just couldn't possibly happen; it is too awful to contemplate. We should also remember that every country that entered the First World War did so in the supreme certainty that they were defending their nation. This is precisely the line that members of the twenty first century nuclear club use to justify their ownership of their weapons. India and Pakistan, North and South Korea and the other powers are morally convinced that they will never use their weapons except to retaliate. In addition there is the problem of nationalism. As I keep arguing, nationalism in its minor key is more than acceptable, but in its extreme form it can be explosive, unpredictable and, as in the case of the Third Reich, hugely destructive. "My country right or wrong" can never be a justification for aggression. Add to this the possibility of terrorists getting their hands on even a limited nuclear device and the future really does seem bleak.

So a brief glance into hell is my recipe for avoiding the unthinkable and this is what the world might look like if a conflagration ever did break out.

The bombs detonated by the US over Hiroshima and Nagasaki were 15 kilotons. This is roughly the size of the ones now in the hands of India, Pakistan and North Korea and within the capability of being used by terrorist groups if they were able to obtain one. Outlined below is the effects just one of those bombs can have. It should be remembered that twenty first century ones are many times more powerful.

There are five outcomes of a nuclear detonation:

Firstly a blast wave, travelling several times faster than sound, demolishes buildings up to two kilometres away from the explosion and there will be few survivors. Further away the blast has the power of a cyclone. Unprotected humans will be hurled against walls and furniture and will suffer serious injuries.

Secondly there are the thermal effects. The temperature at the core of the explosion is similar to that at the centre of the sun so that everything near the ground instantly vaporises. The remaining gases of the bomb and other material form a rising fireball which rises like a balloon, eventually forming the familiar mushroom shaped cloud as it rises and cools.

The third effect is radiation. The debris spilling out of the mushroom cloud is highly radioactive. Depending on winds, this fallout can disperse over vast distances. After the Chernobyl accident in 1986, for example, British farmers in the UK, over two thousand miles away, had to destroy radioactive sheep. Experts have forecast that the immediate area surrounding the Chernobyl factory will be contaminated for at least two thousand years. Of course natural radiation is present in the atmosphere but at relatively low levels. It is measured in a unit called rem. Acceptable levels for workers occasionally exposed to radiation are 5 rem per year and an average x ray is about 0.08 rem so not much danger there. If you are exposed to high levels, however, as will be the case in a nuclear war, then 1000 rems will mean you will have an 80% chance of contracting cancer.

Fourthly there is the problem of radiation producing highly charged electromagnetic fields which can wipe out computers, TVs, radios and crucial communication centres. In the aftermath of an explosion there would be zero chance of restoring links to the outside world. In fact military experts have calculated that a powerful nuclear bomb could probably destroy the whole communication systems of an entire country.

Finally there are the effects on climate: A nuclear war would create massive amounts of smoke which could linger in the stratosphere for ten years or more. This would prevent sunlight from reaching large parts of the world and would also destroy much of the protective ozone layer, thus allowing lethal amounts of UV light to flood in. The overall result would be a massive drop in temperature, with loss of sunlight and drastically reduced growing seasons. The world would return to an ice age and mass starvation and extinction of humans and animals would follow.

The world stood on the cliff edge of this hell on October 1962 when the Soviet Union and the US found themselves on a nuclear collision course in the Atlantic Ocean. I was a young boy at the time but I remember vividly my parents and older relatives clustered around the radio as they listened in to the terrifying crisis developing. The Russian president Khrushchev had decided to catch up in the arms race by positioning Soviet missiles on Cuba, only a few hundred miles from US cities. This was really in response to American positionings of their own missiles in Turkey, within striking range of Russian cities. Kennedy warned Khrushchev to remove the missiles, but when there was no response he set up a naval blockade in the Atlantic, directly in the path of a Soviet convoy which was carrying more missiles to Cuba. The two sides refused to back down, neither wishing to be the one seen to "blink" first. There were frantic behind the scenes diplomatic initiatives but the situation worsened when news came through that a Soviet nuclear submarine was going to block the path of an American aircraft carrier. This was brinkmanship on a cataclysmic scale.

John Kennedy's brother Robert remembered that when the president heard this news he turned grey and his fist went up to his mouth in horror. He knew that if the submarine attacked he would have to order a return strike and launch four thousand warheads. The Soviet submarine stayed silent, withdrew into the black Atlantic depths and I believe Kennedy must have said a private prayer in relief and the world breathed again.

The nuclear situation now is vastly different. In 1962 the two power blocks both knew that neither could win. Even if there were a first strike the response from the defending country would still be devastating and mutual destruction would be the result. Now, in the early part of the twenty first century, there are rogue states, terrorist organisations and border tensions, any one of which could trigger off a nuclear conflict. Here, for example, is Chairman Mao of China toying with the idea of a possible nuclear war while addressing the Communist world's leaders in 1957:

"If war broke out how many people would die? There are 2.7 billion people in the entire world. If the worst came to the worst, perhaps one half would die. But there would still be one half left; imperialism would be razed to the ground and the whole world would become socialist. After a number of years, the world's population would once again reach 2.7 billion and certainly become bigger."

These were chilling words expressing his conviction that to achieve an earthly paradise, in this case a socialist one, then the ends would justify the means. Hitler was very much of the same mind and would have had no hesitation in using nuclear bombs if they had been within reach. He was once asked if he regretted the huge loss of life that the two world wars had led to and his response was equally appalling: "Man uberlebt es." In other words mankind would just about endure. It would "overlive" it.

In 2017 there are, thankfully, no Chairman Maos or Hitlers with their fingers on a nuclear button but there are renegade states, religious fanatics, terrorists and extreme nationalists who might just be mad enough to use them. It is therefore the responsibility of all of us to ensure that common sense, vigilance and intelligent diplomacy play their rightful part in preventing Armageddon. We cannot repeat the mistakes of the past, when extreme nationalism was allowed to run unchallenged. Future generations will never forgive us if we forget.

Chapter Four

GLOBAL TRUST DEFICIT

As a result of JASTA there could be a universal political crisis as countries seek to defend themselves from legal challenges. Additional tension in particular is prevalent amongst some African nations who feel that the International Criminal Court (ICC) is bowing to too much subtle pressure from the West. There is trouble brewing in the continent because there is the perception that some of their leaders are being deliberately targeted. They feel aggrieved because many African countries played a formative role in the negotiation of the Rome Statute, which in turn led to the formation of the ICC itself. They gave their full and optimistic support to its formation, as did the African Non-Governmental organisations (NGOs).

There was understandable dismay, therefore, in 2000 when an arrest warrant for Abdoulaye Y. Ndombasi was issued. At the time Ndombasi was the Minister of Foreign Affairs in the Democratic Republic of the Congo and the initiative from Belgium shattered the level of trust that had previously existed between the two countries as it encroached on the issue of sovereign protection. The relationship was damaged even further in 2008 when Rose Kabuye, the Chief of Protocol to President Paul Kagame of Rwanda, was arrested in Germany following a warrant from a French court. The French alleged that Kabuye had been complicit in the shooting down of the plane, and consequent deaths, of the former Presidents of Rwanda and Burundi, Juvenal Habyarima and Cyprian Ntayamira, in 1994. President Kagame took the issue to the UN claiming that European nations were humiliating African leaders and also threatened to arrest French nationals living in his country (Plessis, Maluwa and O'Reilly 2013, pp.3-4).

Friction also arose between the ICC and the African Union (AU) in 2009 when the court issued the first arrest warrant for President Omar Bashir of Sudan. To make matters worse there was also an obligation imposed on other African nations to arrest him if ever he visited their countries. This mandate, however, has been ignored by the said countries (Plessis, Maluwa and O'Reilly 2013, pp 3-4). It is obvious, therefore, that any increased pressure to comply with the JASTA Act will only worsen relationships between the US and other countries and increase the likelihood of intensifying the growth of nationalism as these countries seek to protect themselves from outside interference.

One of the most alarming developments on the international scene is the deteriorating relationship between NATO and Russia, which is undergoing a revival of nationalism under President Putin. Since the end of the Cold War in 1990, the two sides had been edging closer together in mutual understanding. In fact Russia became a member of the North Atlantic Cooperation Council in 1991 and the Partnership for Peace programme three years later. Further warming of the relationship followed in 2002 when the NATO-Russia Council (NRC) was formed. Since then President Putin, perhaps sensing a weakening of resolve in the Western democracies, has been engaged in a massive military build-up of his forces. In response to his rhetoric, and deployment of troops on Russia's European borders, Sweden recently signed a defence pact with the US, and Finland is following behind. As many as 30,000 newly formed Russian motorised rifle brigades have been positioned close to the Lithuanian border and short range missiles that can carry nuclear weapons have been delivered to areas within striking distance of all European capital cities. Russia's annexing of the Crimea and attempts to do the same to Ukraine is fresh in the memory, as is the recent launching of a battle fleet of ships into the Mediterranean in support of the bombing campaign in Syria.

The annexing of territory in the Crimea was in violation of Article 2(4) of the UN Charter and the International Security architecture. The German Chancellor, Angela Merkel, argued during the Munich Security Conference in 2015 that there should be no attempt to alter any European borders and that Russia's actions needed to be challenged and checked.

In response to all this the Russians described their military build-up as a reply to NATO exercises and to the West's offering Ukraine membership of NATO, which they see as encroaching too close to their territorial interests. Studies by the Rand Corporation for the Pentagon have concluded that Estonia and Latvia would be in Russian hands in as little as 36 hours and that it would be impossible for NATO to do anything about it as it would take too much time to invoke Article 5 of its charter for mutual defence.

It is well documented that the Russian economy is in trouble and opinion both within and outside Russia is convinced that any war with the West would be a disaster. It is interesting also that the two men seem to have respect for each other, recognising perhaps their mutual pragmatism, belief in nationalism and strong leadership qualities.

Here is President Trump on President Putin in July 2016:

"I would treat Vladimir Putin firmly, but there's nothing I can think of that I'd rather do than have Russia friendly as opposed to how they are right now so we can go and knock out Isis, together with other people. Wouldn't it be nice if we actually got along?"

And President Putin on President Trump in December 2015:

"He is a very flamboyant man, very talented, no doubt about that... He is an absolute leader of the Presidential race, as we see it today. He says that he wants to move to another level of relations with Russia. How can we not welcome that? Of course we welcome it."

There was applause in the Russian Parliament when President Trump's election victory was announced on November 9th, 2016 where he is viewed as a political realist whom President Putin can do business with, and it should be remembered that the economic sanctions were imposed by President Obama's executive order and therefore a new president could withdraw them without consulting Congress.

These exchanges and responses have set alarm bells ringing in the top echelons of NATO. The transatlantic treaty has guaranteed peace in Europe since 1945 and has been a permanent counter to any Russian expansionist moves into the Baltic States and Ukraine, but President Trump has been grumbling that some of the member countries have not been pulling their weight. The US contributes 70% of the NATO budget and has by far the most powerful forces but frustration is growing. He is deliberately pointing his finger at those member countries which have not met the minimum requirement of 2 per cent of national income to maintain the upkeep of the alliance.

Article 5 of the NATO Treaty states that an attack on one of the 22 member countries is an attack on all and any undermining of that pledge would be disastrous for European security. It will be interesting to see if a threat to withdraw US defensive cover would prompt those countries to start contributing their fair share of the budget.

In addition there is growing concern in Ukraine at any possible rapprochement between President Putin and President Trump. President Poroshenko offered his sincere congratulations to him on his election victory but asked for continued US support "in our fight against Russian aggression".

Following on from President Trump's election victory and his worries about the relevance of NATO there were voices being heard in the EU, notably from Mr Juncker, that it was maybe time to think about the formation of a European army. Consequent objections to even voicing an opinion like that could reduce the importance of the Alliance in the eyes of President Trump; also, all 22 NATO allies should be doing all they can to convince him that the alliance is not there just for the security and stability of Europe but for the US as well. In which case they should immediately make sure that the minimum requirement of 2% of their budget goes where it should go. It also goes without saying that the formation of a strictly European defence force would be highly problematic, given the already deep divisions and nationalistic movements that are beginning to stir in many of the member countries.

Chapter Five

THE ARAB SPRING AND RELATED INTERNATIONAL IMPLICATIONS

It was a sunny December morning in 2010 in Sidi Bouzid, Tunisia, and twenty six year old Mohamed Bouazizi was setting up his vegetable stall in the central market. There were hundreds of young men like him, many with university degrees, spending much of their day loitering in cafes in the impoverished town, three hundred kilometres south of the capital Tunis, wondering if they would ever find work. Bouazizi didn't have a degree, but he did have an ambition to raise enough money to buy or rent a pick-up truck to expand his fledgling business. He would never be rich; on a good day he might make about seven dollars, but he was proud to be the breadwinner for his widowed mother and six siblings.

What happened next would eventually send the Arab world into turmoil. A policewoman walked up to his stall and confiscated his unlicensed vegetable cart and all his goods. Bouazizi tried to pay the seven dinar fine, which for him represented a full day's work, but she allegedly insulted his dead father, slapped him and spat in his face. Something in Bouazizi snapped. The public humiliation and the loss of his business were just too much to bear. When the local officials refused to hear his complaints he poured fuel over himself and set himself on fire right outside their offices at 11.30

a.m. He died later from his burns in hospital on January 4th.

There was a huge public outcry and, sensing a pivotal moment in the country's mood, even President Zine el Abidine Ben Ali visited him to show his concern. After nearly a month of protests, however, and with no let-up in the public outcry, he accepted the advice of his generals and fled the country he had ruled for twenty four years.

Bouazizi became a legend. Within weeks there were more young people setting themselves on fire in several Arab cities, including Cairo and Algiers, in protest against corruption, high unemployment and dictatorial rule. Demonstrations erupted in Egypt, Libya, Syria, Yemen, Bahrain and Jordan. Long simmering frustrations over poverty, human rights, police violence and the greed of political elites shook governments to their foundations. Back in Sidi Bouzid Mohamed's mother Mannoubia was racked by grief but she was proud of her son. "Although I am in mourning and I am sad, thanks to God, Mohamed lives, he didn't die. He lives on, his name lives on. I am proud of what happened in Tunis. I am proud that he is known throughout the Arab world."

The people of Bouzid echoed her feelings. In a street near Mohamed's home the graffiti reads "This is the location of the revolution".

It really was a revolution as democratic uprisings flared throughout North Africa and the Middle East. In January 2011 President Hosni Mubarak was forced out of office following huge demonstrations in Tahrir Square in Cairo. In February there were protests in Libya when five human rights lawyers were arrested by Colonel Gaddafi. In the same month the UN Security Council passed a no fly zone over Libya and days later naval vessels and warplanes began to bomb Gaddafi's forces eventually resulting in his flight from office and eventual capture and killing. Government forces in Syria shot dead five protestors in the southern city of Deraa, igniting the beginning of a large scale uprising against President Bashar al-Assad. By October there were estimates of three thousand casualties and fears of an open civil war. In June Yemeni's President Ali Abdullah Saleh was wounded in a bomb attack on his palace in the capital city of Sana. Later, after hundreds of demonstrators had been killed, he was ousted and overthrown.

These were cataclysmic events but there were only short term gains. Hopes were raised in Tunisia and Egypt where free and fair elections were held after the existing regimes had been replaced, but there was a form of counter revolution in Egypt when Abdel Fattah el-Sisi overthrew the elected Muslim Brotherhood government in a military coup in July 2013. Elsewhere there were token attempts at reform and the more stable monarchies of Morocco and the Gulf States were able to maintain social order without crashing into civil war.

What was apparent to many was that the Arab Spring was perceived by some as turning into the Arab Winter. Despite hopeful assurances from France and the UK, Libya broke up into factional tribal fighting and Syria finally sank into its own chaotic civil war. In Iraq there was the rise of Isis and its vow to turn the whole region into a powerful Caliphate, accompanied by an apocalyptic showdown with the "crusader" forces of the West.

As a result of the political turmoil and violence there is a huge refugee problem facing Europe as thousands of Libyans, Syrians and Tunisians risk their lives to find safety. The ones who are gambling their lives are mainly young men and the talented, energetic types who would be vital to their own country's future progress if life there was more stable.

It remains to be seen whether countries can absorb these masses and integrate them into their own societies. In the first six months of 2015 Sweden took in 75,000 refugees and in 2016 500,000 arrived on the shores of Italy and Greece. This has been a godsend for the far right political groups who argue that there just isn't enough money or jobs to go round, particularly when there is already a huge unemployment crisis in both these countries. Ominously in Sweden, which has an honourable record of absorbing political refugees, the Swedish Democratic party, on the right of the political spectrum, has seen its support grow from 7.5% to 25% in the last five years. In Austria the far right Freedom Party almost captured Vienna's mayorality in 2015 and in 2016 the far right candidate Norbert Hofer was only narrowly defeated in the Head of State election; and in France Marine Le Pen, who calls herself "Madame Frexit", has distanced herself from her allegedy racist, xenophobic father and is now leading the presidential field with 35% of the potential vote.

Moreover, many of these parties look to Greece and its never ending economic woes as proof that the EU is a troubled project. Its unemployment rate is twenty six per cent and just one recent bailout cost the EU taxpayers ninety eight billion dollars. The obvious question that is being asked is how long can Greece remain a member of the EU if it cannot address its recurrent financial crises.

My preoccupation is that that these reflex reactions and developments could lead to a retreat into a narrow form of nationalism, even the break-up of the EU. The consequent fragmentation of society, as ethnic groups, fearful for their safety, bond with each other in mutual suspicion, would be a cause for deep alarm.

Another problem for Europe is its precarious financial position. Unless you are German, or maybe British, the economic outlook is very gloomy. When Russia annexed the Crimea, the US imposed economic sanctions, which in turn cost the EU billions of dollars in lost trade. Russia is the US's twenty third largest trade partner but it is Europe's third. The German magazine "Die Welt" forecast that economic sanctions on Russia could cost Europe one hundred and fourteen billion dollars and up to two million lost jobs.

Then there is the problem of gas. Russia exports about one hundred and fifty million cubic metres of it to Europe, mostly to Germany and the UK; taking into account other southern European countries, it provides thirty per cent of the continent's needs and it can turn off the taps any time it wants. True, it would cost Russia lost revenue, but it would also make life very hard indeed in the customer countries' winter months when reserve stocks would expire.

In the wider world President Putin knows the importance of maintaining Russia's influence in the Middle East and that if he can reverse the flow of refugees into Europe by stabilising Syria, many member countries would breathe more easily and he would have won more allies. This in turn could undermine European unity and affect the trans-Atlantic accord in his favour. This is one reason why Brexit has so alarmed many of the EU leadership who see the future of their project under direct threat of disintegration.

Add to the scenario the as yet untested aspirations of President Trump and once more the international scene begins to resemble the confusions and uncertainties of the late nineteenth and early twentieth centuries that eventually led to World War One.

Chapter Six

THE CIVIL WAR IN SYRIA AND THE CONFLICT BETWEEN PAKISTAN AND INDIA

In 2011, during "The Arab Spring", peaceful protests gathered pace in Syria, as in other neighbouring countries. The security services clamped down on them ruthlessly, imprisoning fifteen boys who had dared to write graffiti in support of the Spring. According to Al Jazeera, one of the boys, thirteen year old Hamza al-Khateeb, died after undergoing severe torture when detained by the Airforce intelligence services. When his body was returned to his parents his mother was prevented from seeing his body. His father looked, fainted in disbelief at the marks of burns and beatings, and vowed revenge.

The Assad Government's response to the protests was the killing of hundreds of demonstrators and imprisonment of many more. In July of the same year defectors from the military wing of the government formed a breakaway rebel group called the Free Syrian Army. A civil war had begun.

It had been a long time growing. For years Syrians had been complaining bitterly about corruption, high levels of unemployment and a lack of political freedom. President Assad, who had succeeded his father Havez in 2000, promised wide-ranging reforms, including a move to root level democracy and a fight against corruption. Hundreds of political prisoners were released from jail and independent newspapers began to publish again after "disappearing" for more than thirty years. There was even a blind eye turned to groups of intellectuals who were allowed to hold debates and public meetings.

The freedoms didn't last very long. Assad and his government were suspicious of the growing influence of Islamist and Kurdish activists, and arrests and long prison sentences followed. The freedom of the press was curtailed and there was a feeling in the country that the "old Guard", members of the Government who had been loyal to his father and other close relatives, had significant influence over him. He also introduced the hated "emergency powers" which permitted the security forces to arrest and torture at will.

His hard line policies towards Israel and his criticism of the 2003 invasion of Iraq, led by a US coalition, did win him many friends in the wider world, but suspicions that he had been somehow involved in the assassination of Lebanon's former Prime Minister Rafik Hariri in 2005 provoked international condemnation, despite his vigorous denials of involvement. Consequently, a reluctant Assad had to withdraw his forces from Lebanon, ending a twenty nine year old "presence".

In March 2011 anti-government protests in the southern city of Deraa convinced Assad that insurgents and saboteurs were deliberately undermining his attempts at reforms and economic progress. He responded with a ruthless show of force, dismissed his cabinet, and sent in troops supported by tanks into city centres. His reply to international criticism was that he was combating armed criminal gangs who were attempting to undermine the stability of the country. There was also the fact ISIS were beginning to take control over vast parts of Syria and Iraq.

When the conflict spread to all parts of the country, regional and world powers started to intervene, complicating an already chaotic scenario. Iran, Russia, Saudi Arabia and the US surveyed the situation and took sides, offering military and financial support wherever they saw fit, and what had once been a secular country started to divide along religious and sectarian lines.

Russia, wanting to maintain its influence in the region, gave open backing to Assad, launching bombing strikes against rebel-held positions and also against those of ISIS, the jihadist extremists who had pounced on the divisions of the country as a preliminary to their visions of a Caliphate that would shatter the existing borders of the entire Middle East. Russia stressed that it would target only rebel-held areas, but in late 2016 they were coming under fierce international criticism because of their apparent disregard for inflicting civilian casualties in the process. Shia-dominated Iran also had an ulterior motive in assisting the Alawite Assad forces. By sending in military advisors, weapons and troops on the ground, Iran was fully aware this would guarantee its shipments of weapons across Syria to reach the Shia Islamist movement Hezbollah in and around Lebanon.

The US was more cautious in its approach, initially accusing Assad's forces of committing atrocities and then offering non-lethal aid such as food rations and transport vehicles to the more moderate rebel groups, such as the Free Syrian Army. They later began to offer more practical help, such as intelligence reports and financial aid to carefully selected Syrian rebel commanders. Then they started to turn their attention to the growing threat posed by ISIS. In September 2014 President Obama made no secret of his determination to seek out and destroy ISIS: "I have made it clear that we will hunt down terrorists who threaten our country, wherever they are." Later that month a formidable alliance of the US, Bahrain, Jordan, Qatar, Saudi Arabia and the United Arab

Emirates began air strikes, not just against ISIS but also against the Khorsan group to the west of Aleppo and the al-Nusra Front around Raqqah.

The effects of the war have been catastrophic. More than 4.8 million people, mostly women and children, have fled the country, and Lebanon, Jordan and Turkey are struggling to cope with the largest exodus in living memory. Hundreds of thousands of these people have somehow reached Europe, walking all the way and there is growing anger and worry amongst the Europeans as to which country should accept them. After initially welcoming the refugees with open arms, Angela Merkel is now bowing to public pressure and insisting on more control of the German borders.

In the rebel-held areas the leaders have refused to accept any form of humanitarian aid to the trapped civilians and there are more than four million of them reduced to near starvation levels with a complete lack of medical supplies adding to their plight.

This is bad enough but the most worrying aspect of the war is the prospect of worsening relations between Russia and the US. There is already tension in the air over Russia's territorial claims in Ukraine and its arms build-up on its western borders with Europe. Now Syria can be added to the mix. The US had formerly made no secret of its insistence that Assad and his government had to go before any peace talks could begin, but as the focus shifted onto combating Isis, they found themselves in an unforeseen alliance with Russia. In the battles that followed, the US was seen as very much the weaker partner in the alliance as Russian forces intensified their campaign against the rebels.

On the other hand there has been increasing condemnation in international circles at the indiscriminate nature of the Russian bombing campaign. A UK-based monitoring group called The

Syrian Observatory for Human Rights has reported that about 4000 civilians have been killed in one year of Russian strikes.

If there is going to be an eventual winner in this conflict my instincts tell me that it will be Assad and his Russian backers. The ruthless bombing campaign and the training of the Syrian troops by Russian special forces is having a significant weakening effect on the rebel groups, and the fact that President Trump has already expressed his desire to do business with Putin will ensure that the hard line Russian approach will probably be left to continue.

Whether the relationships between the two powers will flourish in the wider world will depend on the extent of Putin's ambition and the resolve of the US to bolster its NATO allies.

OTHER AREAS OF CONFLICT. PAKISTAN/ INDIA

For about the last seventy years the dispute between Pakistan and India over the territory of Kashmir has threatened the peace of the entire Asian sub-continent and even the world.

The worrying factor is that both countries are in possession of nuclear weapons and neither one has signed the nuclear Non Proliferation Treaty.

India has a stockpile of more than one hundred nuclear warheads and Pakistan about half that number, but these statistics are meaningless considering the apocalyptic havoc that could be caused by just one bomb. So far both sides have kept their hands off the nuclear button, although Pakistan has declared that it has a "first strike" policy, meaning it will not use its nuclear option unless it feels its armed forces are unable to halt an invasion, which nearly happened in the war of 1971. India has a strict policy of "no first use".

What is alarming is that Pakistan is developing what it calls "theatre nuclear weapons", or low yield tactical bombs which could still cause immense damage. If they were to use them then the chances of the conflict spreading would be significantly increased as allied blocks would line up in support. Another fear is that of a militant group somehow getting its hands on a nuclear weapon and deliberately targeting innocent civilians.

During the 1999 border conflict, fought in the Kargil district of Kashmir, the Pakistan Government actually ordered the military to arm its nuclear weapons. Thankfully a truce was negotiated and peace was temporarily restored.

On September 18th, 2016 an attack on an Indian army base, resulted in the death of nineteen soldiers. India retaliated on the 29th when its special forces raided some terrorist launch pads and inflicted casualties. An indication that India didn't want to escalate the crisis but that it felt it had to respond, came when its Director General of Military Operations called on his opposite number in Pakistan to forewarn him that a strike was coming. The subtlety of this message conveyed very clearly that the military response to the raid was meant to be interpreted as a necessary face saving measure and not an attempt to deepen the crisis.

The origins of the conflict go back to the partition of India in the aftermath of the Second World War in 1947. The British Empire was disintegrating and there was pressure to ensure a fair division of the country, if possible along religious and ethnic lines. It should have ended in a peaceful solution but the Muslims and Hindus were randomly scattered throughout India and when the new country of Pakistan was formed there were still about a third of the Muslim population left behind.

There was horrific violence amongst the Muslim, Hindu and Sikh communities with upwards of a million deaths. There were Princely-ruled territories such as Kashmir and Hyderabad which were given the choice of which country they could join. Unfortunately both India and Pakistan laid claim on Kashmir and the area has been a major source of conflict ever since. The Maharaja of Kashmir, Hari Singh, was the Hindu head of a majority Muslim State and couldn't decide which way to go. In 1947, frustrated by his delaying tactics and hearing of reports of attacks on Muslims, tribesmen from Pakistan invaded Kashmir and the Maharaja immediately sent for help from India. India's Governor General at the time was Lord Mountbatten and he decided the best thing to do was to let Kashmir join India on a temporary basis while anticipating a vote on its future. Hari Singh signed an agreement that ceded control of foreign and defence policy to India and Indian troops marched in to take over two thirds of the country, principally in the south, while Pakistan took over the rest.

There has been pressure from Pakistan to hold a referendum to decide the status of Kashmir, while India takes the position that it is already part of India, having taken part in numerous State and national elections. The UN did declare in favour of Pakistan's demand for a referendum but India claims that the Simla Agreement of 1972 commits the two countries to solving the problem between themselves, without the interference of a neutral body.

The impasse or stalemate continues to this day and there are even voices in Kashmir which are calling for it to be independent of both countries.

Bitter, inconclusive conflicts were fought in 1947-48 and 1965, though some stability came when a ceasefire line was agreed upon. This didn't stop further outbreaks in 1999 and again in 2002. Alarm bells had already been ringing in 1989 when an Islamist-led insurgency complicated the politics of the dispute and the terror attacks in Mumbai in 2008 stiffened India's resolve to maintain its hold on its section of Kashmir.

It is a sobering thought that any one of these areas of conflict could quickly reignite and set off a chain reaction in the wider world. Once again it is aggressive nationalism that is the main contributing factor to the tensions and if JASTA becomes a reality then the problem will only intensify.

Chapter Seven

OTHER AREAS OF POTENTIAL CONFLICT. NORTH KOREA, IRAN AND YEMEN, AND SOUTH AMERICA

In the late 1980s and early 1990s the Berlin Wall finally came down and the great communist experiment in the Soviet Union collapsed. Many of the satellite territories recovered their national identities, reintroducing their own currencies and proudly raising their flags. The rebirth of nationalism may sound counterproductive to my argument that it was the rise of extreme nationalism, among other factors, which ushered in the first and second world wars, but I would counter that by adding that there was also an accompanying emphasis on democracy and free speech which ensured brakes on any further move to the right and an aggressive form of nationalism. I would also argue that the disintegration of the monolithic Soviet Union was a huge relief after the cold war tensions of the previous forty years, when the outbreak of a nuclear war with the West was a permanent possibility.

While the Soviet Union collapsed, China remained its enigmatic self, nominally proclaiming its communist ethos, while at the same time allowing the natural engines of state controlled capitalism to power its economy.

The one country that made no concessions to modernisation or reform was North Korea, which stubbornly clung to its isolationism and its inflexible adherence to communist ideology. I mention it because its nuclear ambitions, its separation from the community of nations, and its unpredictable leadership make it difficult to deal with on a diplomatic basis.

The country was formed in 1948, following on from the chaotic international situation at the end of the Second World War and it was dominated by its "Great leader", Kim II-Sung, for almost half a century. He ruled with an iron fist until 1994, clamping down on any signs of dissent. He even changed the international calendar so that the year in North Korea is counted from his birth date (1912). In 2017, therefore, it will be 106. His grandfather was a Protestant Minister and he himself was raised as a Presbyterian but he rejected his Christian beliefs in favour of a strict form of atheistic Marxism. Christmas Day celebrations are forbidden; instead Kim Jong-il's mother's birthday is celebrated instead.

It is a country that is perceived to be in a permanent state of crisis with regular food shortages and even famine, and the regime stands accused of systematic human rights abuses on an epic scale. Amnesty International claims that hundreds of thousands of dissidents and "criminals" are held in detention centres where executions and torture are endemic. The UN has recently warned its current leader Kim Jong-un that North Korea will be referred to the International Criminal Court to answer charges relating to crimes against humanity.

It is considered to be one of the world's most dangerous and unpredictable hotspots because of its determined nuclear ambitions and its isolationist tendencies. It has recently accelerated its testing of its nuclear bombs and missiles and experts predict that it will soon be capable of firing an intercontinental warhead that could reach the west coast of the US.

It is possible that just as Putin is testing the resolve of NATO by conducting manoeuvres on Europe's borders, so the North Koreans might try a similar option to test Trump's strength of purpose. On the other hand Trump has offered to open talks with Kim Jong-un, the son of and successor to Kim Jong-il and this might worry US allies such as South Korea and Japan who would see any softening of approach as a threat to their own security. Apparently he has already made some critical remarks about their not contributing enough to the nuclear umbrella that the US provides, similar to the complaints he made about NATO. Of additional concern is that there is a group of hard-nosed nationalists in South Korea who feel it is time to break ties with the US and start an independent route to gaining their own nuclear weapons.

Another potential flashpoint is Iran, not just because it is fiercely embroiled in supporting the Assad government in the Syrian war, but because it could be on the brink of developing its own nuclear capabilities. In 2015 it signed a deal with six major powers, the US, UK, France, Germany, Russia and China, promising to scale down its nuclear programme in return for international sanctions to be relieved. President Trump has threatened to renege on this deal arguing that more sanctions would lead to more concessions. This is causing understandable alarm in US diplomatic circles which reply that the other five signatory countries would still feel themselves bound by the treaty, so isolating the US and indirectly encouraging Iran to reduce its nuclear concessions.

YEMEN

The conflict in Yemen is in danger of becoming known as the forgotten war. The attention of the world seems to be focussed exclusively on the Syrian conflict but since 2015 more than seven thousand people have been killed and nearly forty thousand injured in this struggling country's civil conflict.

I think it is a mistake to view it as a local problem because the war has the backing of two rival factions, Iran and Saudi Arabia, and there is always the possibility of the violence spreading even further, as happened in the two world wars of the twentieth century. The situation is hugely complicated and it is thought that a dangerous mix of Shia Houthi rebels, Sunni tribes, Saudi Arabia and allied Gulf Arab States, Iran, al Qaeda and Islamic State are involved.

The country has a long history of outside interference. In the nineteen sixties it was ravaged by a civil war and the then Egyptian President Nasser sent his air force in support of the republicans against the royalists. It became a British protectorate until 1967 and then the Soviet Union provided backing to a communist regime until another civil war which ended in 1994.

A simplified explanation of the current conflict would begin with an uprising in 2011 forcing its long-time authoritarian President, Ali Abdullah Saleh, to resign, having promised a handover of power to his deputy, Mr Hadi. He, however, was faced with huge political and social problems, including attacks from al Qaeda in the south of the country, discontent from many military officers still loyal to Mr Saleh, and corruption, unemployment and food shortages.

In the north, the heartland of the Zaidi Shia Muslims, who had previously challenged the Saleh Government with a series of rebellions, trouble was stirring and the Houthi movement seized upon the perceived weakness of Mr Hadi's administration by taking control of vast areas of Saada province.

It should be explained that the Houthis are a minority in Yemen and are opposed not just by the Sunnis in the south, but also by the jihadists of al Qaeda and ISIS who consider them to be heretics. It was then the turn of Isis who entered the battle with their trademark suicide bomb attacks and on the twentieth of March 2015 they targeted four Shia mosques, killing more than one hundred and thirty worshippers. Iran is allegedly supporting the Houthis but this is denied by senior figures in their movement.

This inspired other Yemenis and in September 2014 they entered the capital city of Saana. By January 2015 they had captured it completely, forcing Mr Hadi and his ministers into house arrest. Somehow the new president escaped to the southern port of Aden in the south to set up what he called his legitimate government. This didn't last long as the Houthis, now joined by the security forces still loyal to Mr Saleh, attempted to take control of the entire country.

It was at this point that other powers in the area, alarmed at what they understood to be an Iranian-backed Shia uprising, formed alliances supported with logistics and intelligence by the US, UK and France. Saudi Arabia and a coalition of eight other mostly Arab states then initiated a bombing campaign in the hope of restoring Mr Hadi's legitimate government. A fierce four month battle for the strategic port of Aden in the south was won by forces loyal to President Hadi, while the southern city of Taiz is now under permanent siege from the rebels who continue to fire shells across the border into Saudi Arabia.

The UN has been able to make assessments of the conflict and they make very disturbing reading, as it is the innocent and powerless who are suffering most. Almost half the population is under eighteen and that number accounts for a third of all civilian deaths. It reports that approximately fourteen million people are facing drastic food shortages and almost half a million children are at risk of starving to death.

At the present moment it seems that no side is capable of ending the war, but if that is the case then it is quite possible that a major push from either the Houthis or the Government forces could involve the various coalitions on a wider scale, just as the Balkan war trip-started the First World War in 1914. It should also be remembered that Yemen, and particularly the port of Aden, is of crucial strategic importance because it guards the Bab al-Mandab Strait, a narrow waterway linking the Gulf of Aden with the Red Sea. This is where the oil tankers of the world manoeuvre their way to Europe and beyond, a lifeline for the global economy. Aden is now the base of President Hadi and he has made a direct appeal to the Gulf Cooperation Council (GCC) for a military intervention and an imposition of a no fly zone to reduce the tension.

So far the war has been contained within the southern Arabian peninsula but the danger is that a stalemate could involve a major initiative and the resulting escalation might draw in the major international powers, particularly if they see that their jugular vein, the oil pipeline, is under threat of a takeover or closure.

Further afield in Central and South America there is little to fear from a nuclear conflict but in certain parts the long term problems of poverty, crime, political instability and environmental crises continue. According to the UN the gap between the continent's rich and poor is the widest in the world, with the top 20% of the wealthy holding 57% of all resources. There are border conflicts between Columbia on the one hand and Ecuador and Venezuela on the other, and Columbian guerrilla fighters are currently ignoring a ceasefire pact, but the chances of South America somehow triggering international conflicts is a bit remote.

What is very clear, however, is that in South America populism, the Donald Trump anti liberal establishment phenomenon that is sweeping most of the rest of the world, is in full retreat. Only a few years ago it was the national populists who held sway over most of the continent. Now, Venezuela's Hugo Chavez is dead, Argentina's Ms Fernandez is out of office and facing corruption charges, Bolivia's Evo Morales has lost a referendum and Ecuador's Rafael Correa has resigned. These were all Donald Trump like figures, posing as saviours of the people, who promised reforms, an end to corruption and high investment. They never happened. To maintain popularity these leaders borrowed and borrowed, but inflation eroded wages and economic stagnation was the result. The lesson was a painful one to learn and it will be interesting to see if Donald Trump's advisors are noting how the grand promises of populism have to be followed through.

Marcus Tullius Cicero
(106 BCE-44 BCE)

"To be ignorant of what occurred before you is to be always a child."

Orator and statesman who lived at the time of the disintegration of the Roman republic circa 42 BCE. Champion and founder of "The Natural Law", an understanding that a divine providence was at work in the universe providing the key components of reason and eternal religious truths to mankind forming the basic pillars of constitutional democracy. Executed on the orders of Mark Antony.

**Marcus Antonius (Mark Antony)
(83 BCE-31 BCE)**

*Played a critical role in the transformation of
the Roman Republic. Supporter of the young
Octavius Caesar who eventually became the first
emperor, Augustus Caesar; in effect one of its
primary dictators*

Assassination of Archduke Ferdinand and his wife

On June 28th, 1914 Archduke Ferdinand of Austria and his wife Sophie were assassinated by a Serbian nationalist, 16 year old Gavrilo Princip. The photo shows Princip's arrest, seconds after he fired the fatal shots that eventually precipitated the First World War

World War 1

British troops in action during the First World War

World War 1

General Girond's French army attacking German lines towards the end of the war

World War 1

*The invention of the tank in 1918 helped to bring the war
to a conclusion. Its appearance terrified the German infantry*

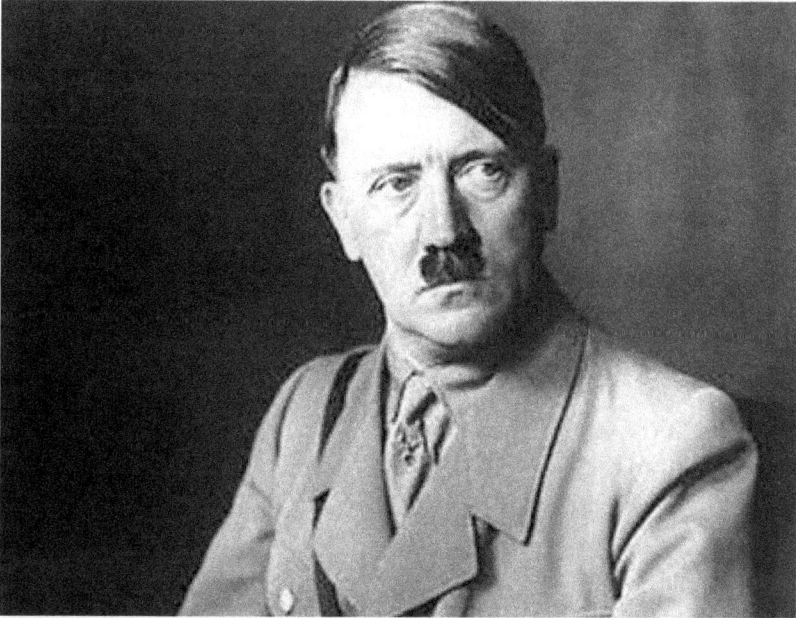

Adolf Hitler
(1889-1945)

Chancellor of Germany from 1935 and thereafter dictator, racist and radical leader of the Nazi party who almost single handedly brought the world close to destruction during the 1939-1945 war. He was a dynamic and charismatic speaker but his invasion of Poland and then Russia sealed his fate, as alliances against him meant his armies had to fight on two huge fronts. He survived at least three assassination attempts but ultimately committed suicide as the Russian Red Army closed in on Berlin in 1945

Benito Mussolini
(1883-1945)

The founder of Italian Fascism and an influence on and ally of Adolf Hitler. He did make the trains run on time but led the country into a series of military disasters. He and his mistress Claretta Petacci were shot by Italian partisans just before the end of the Second World War

**Josef Stalin
(1878-1945)**

*His name meant "man of steel". He helped
defeat Nazism but he lived up to his name,
killing and starving to death millions of
Soviet citizens in his regime of terror*

Mao Zedong
(1873-1976)

Chinese communist leader who ordered
"The great leap forward" and the Cultural
Revolution which allegedly led to famine,
the deaths of millions and the destruction
of much of the country's cultural heritage

World War 2

The Japanese attack on Pearl Harbor on the 7th December 1941 brought America into the war

World War 2

US troops advancing towards Omaha beach, June 1944. The Normandy invasion by allied troops opened up a second front, threatening Hitler's control of occupied Europe. Within a year they and the Russians in the East had reached Berlin and ended his reign of terror

World War 2

The big three. Churchill, Roosevelt and Stalin at the Yalta conference, February 1945. The war is coming to an end and they are discussing an uncertain future. Though they are all smiling, Churchill felt himself to be very much the junior partner and that the other two were excluding him from the crucial decisions

Nuclear Bomb

"Now I am become death, the destroyer of worlds." J.Robert Oppenheimer, the father of the atomic bomb, quoted these words from the Bhagavad Gita when he witnessed the first controlled explosion. Modern atomic bombs are hundreds of times more powerful that the ones dropped on Nagasaki and Hiroshima in 1945

Nuclear Bomb Effects

The horrific aftermath of the second atomic bomb dropped on Nagasaki, August 9, 1945. Together with the earlier bomb on Hiroshima the total number of casualties reached at least 129,000

Nelson Mandela
(1918-2013)

Imprisoned for 27 years for plotting to overthrow the pro-apartheid government in 1962, Nelson Mandela became a hero to people all over the world. He was the first black president of South Africa and gained universal acclaim for championing human rights and for the graceful magnanimity he showed to those who had held him captive. A monumental African leader and an inspiration to future generations

Chapter Eight

ISRAELI/PALESTINIAN DISPUTE

An English teacher friend of mine and his wife were having an
evening meal with a Palestinian family in an Arab country. They
were enjoying themselves as the talk turned to children, school and
holidays and when they would be returning to England. Suddenly,
and for no reason, the Palestinian father asked a question. "Why
do you think people in the West support Israel?" There was
no aggression in the question; he was just being curious. The
Englishman looked to his wife but she shook her head as if to say "I
don't want to get involved".

He thought for a moment and came up with an answer. "You
know, when I was younger I read a book called "Exodus". It was
about the mass Jewish emigration to Palestine from Europe after
the holocaust. I think in Europe there is still a lot of guilt about
what happened to the six million dead."

"You don't believe that, do you?"

"Yes I do."

There was silence and then the Palestinian mother turned to her
husband and said, "Perhaps it's time someone wrote a book about
our exodus…"

I think that little story captures the tragedy and essence of the Palestinian and Israeli conflict. Both sides have their story to tell and, without wanting to express a controversial opinion, I am passionate about finding a long term, durable solution to the problem.

Whatever the interpretation of the facts there is always impasse, outrage and confusion. Each side is utterly convinced that the other is in denial and both have enough "facts" to support their case ten times over.

I have hope in the future, however, for two reasons and the connecting word is "harmony".

The first occurred during my time as Director General of a UN agency. One of my proudest achievements was in bringing to Switzerland groups of young Palestinians and Israelis under the context of training opportunities. The two groups had no idea that they would be working together and at first there was mutual suspicion and tension. Over time this began to disappear and after a few weeks of discussions and team projects they parted as friends, promising to become pioneers in global healing. They had had the patience to listen to the other side's point of view and had developed an understanding that if there was to be a way forward it would never be through violence and hatred. It would be through dialogue, honesty in admitting faults and failures, and a sincere hope that coexistence was an achievable reality and not a naïve fantasy. Such investment in future generations I believe is critical to global healing.

The second reason I have hope is the example of the world famous conductor and pianist Daniel Barenboim, and the late Edward Said, a Palestinian-American. They have achieved even greater things on a huge scale with their West Eastern Divan Orchestra, formed in 1999. This started out as a workshop for musicians from Egypt, Spain, Iran, Israel, Jordan, Lebanon, Palestine and Syria and its primary aim was to replace ignorance with education, knowledge and understanding; to humanize the other and to imagine a better future. Individuals who had only experienced each other through the caricatures of hate suddenly found themselves working together as equals. For the first time in their lives they began to listen and edge closer to each other across the deep chasms of religious and political divides and for many of them, the classical music that was performed seemed to transcend their human perceptions and lift them into more tranquil, eternal realms.

It was music in defiance of war, the triumph of art over hatred and this experiment in coexistence, which was initially a one-off event, became a permanent and legendary reality. The orchestra now performs all over the world to magnificent acclaim.

I am making particular mention of this because the success of the orchestra in bringing together people of differing political opinions is a powerful metaphor for eventual reconciliation and healing. It reminds me of the story of Lenin who denied himself the pleasure of listening to Beethoven because the beauty of the music so harmonised and reconciled him to the world that he wanted afterwards to pat children on the head. He considered this a shocking weakness in a man whose philosophy was based on the liberating power of violence.

Barenboim, who holds both an Israeli and Palestinian passport as a mark of his neutrality, instinctively understands this and is passionate about the transformational effect of classical music upon the human soul, regardless of its religion or nationality. He views the orchestra as a human laboratory that can express to the whole world how to cope with one another.

He was born in Buenos Aires in 1942 and gave his first recital there at the age of only seven. Two years later the family moved to Israel where he made his first recording. His career blossomed and he is now considered to be one of the foremost musicians of the last fifty years.

He is acutely conscious of the suffering that permeates the country. "I suffer from the fact that on the one hand I went to Israel as a child, I grew up there. I went to school there... and I am obviously conscious of our history, being Jewish... And I suffer because I think that so much of what we do, and what has been done is not worthy of that history. People have been creative here for sixty years but I see something that is so thoughtless, and, frankly, stupid as to make the myth of Jewish intelligence totally ungraspable." He couldn't believe that after the partition of Palestine in 1947 there was a war which gave the victorious Israelis the chance to show magnanimity to the Palestinians. Instead, in his opinion, they did nothing and missed a golden opportunity for reconciliation. "There was not a willingness or capacity to see the logic of the other side, even without agreeing with it. It was just a total ignorance of the possibility of another point of view."

It happened again after the six day war in 1967 and the occupation of the Palestinian territories which left the Israelis in charge of huge tracts of land, including the West Bank and Gaza. "Now I have my questions about Jewish intelligence. We say we want a Jewish state. Why do we hold on to territories where there are no Jews and then artificially settle them with people that come, most of them, solely for that fact, to create a physical presence which is nothing more than a justification for having a foot in them? Because of all this I suffer."

He balances this criticism of Israel by conceding that there are faults on the other side, arguing that it would be very difficult to find a Palestinian or an Arab who accepted even the existence of the state of Israel. He sees the conflict in human rather than political terms as one of two people who sincerely believe they have the right to live on the same piece of land and the idea of a military solution as impossible. He thinks there are three scenarios. The first is that both sides kill each other, or they live in a bi-national state, separate but equal, or they form a federal system where there are two states with open borders.

He is realistic about the long term influence that his orchestra can have in helping to achieve any of these aims. "You can't make peace with an orchestra but you can create the conditions for understanding and awaken the curiosity of each individual to listen to the narrative of the other. I'm trying to create a platform where the two sides can disagree and not resort to knives. It is a project against ignorance, a project against the fact that it is absolutely essential for people to get to know the other, to understand what the other thinks and feels, without necessarily agreeing with it. I'm not trying to convert the Arab members of the orchestra to the Israeli point of view, and I'm not trying to convince the Israelis of the Arab point of view."

So the metaphor for peace is there; the very existence of the orchestra is a tantalising vision of what could happen if the guns and bombs were put away and people concentrated on the insanity of the anguish and suffering, admitting that enough was enough, as they did in Northern Ireland and South Africa in recent memory.

One more pointer of hope was the previously mentioned but short lived "Arab Spring". The uprisings in The Middle East and in Egypt, Libya, Tunisia and Syria in particular, evolved out of people's frustrations with government by dictatorship. I believe that deep in the human psyche there is an instinct for political freedom, for free speech, for an independent press, and for an honest legal system that puts corrupt politicians in jail.

It is now fifty years since the Middle East war of June 1967 and there have been many attempts to forge peace plans to end the conflict. There were agreements and recognition between Egypt, Israel and Jordan but the essential settlement, between Israel and Palestine, has not been reached.

A brief summary of the major initiatives might help to clarify the situation and even act as a pointer to ways forward in the future.

After the 1967 war the UN Council Resolution called for "a withdrawal of Israeli armed forces from territories occupied in the recent conflict". The ambiguity of the English word territories caused confusion as the Israelis read it as some, not all territories, while the Arab negotiators argued that it was all territories. Also it was written under Chapter VI of the UN Charter where resolutions are recommendations not orders.

Other peace plans followed but came to nothing and it wasn't until well after the 1973 Yom Kippur War that more initiatives began to be realised. In 1978 US President Jimmy Carter invited President Sadat of Egypt and the Israeli Prime Minister, Menachim Begin, for talks at the Presidential retreat at **Camp David**. President Sadat had already made a historic visit to Jerusalem in 1977, thereby recognising the State of Israel as a reality and indirectly sealing his own death warrant, as he was assassinated in October 1981. After twelve days of talks there were two agreements signed but, crucially, the Palestinians were not involved in either of them. Israel did, however, agree to a withdrawal from the occupied Sinai Peninsula and there was official recognition of the State of Israel and its right to exist.

Encouraged by the success of the Egypt-Israeli treaty, the former

Soviet Union and the US set up a conference in Madrid in 1991, inviting other Arab countries to sign their own agreements with Israel. This time the Palestinians were present, but only as part of a joint delegation with Jordan. Objections from Israel had meant that Yasser Arafat, the leader of the Palestinian Liberation Organisation (PLO), was absent from the talks. A peace treaty between Israel and Jordan was signed but only limited progress was made with other Arab States.

Two years later there was hope that a dramatic breakthrough could be achieved in secret talks in **Oslo** in 1993 and Yasser Arafat was finally invited to take part. An agreement was signed on the White House lawn on September the thirteenth of that year. There is a historic photograph showing Bill Clinton, Yasser Arafat and the Israeli Prime Minister, Yitzak Rabin, smiling and shaking hands.

According to the Oslo Agreement, Israeli troops would withdraw in stages from the West Bank and the Gaza Strip, coinciding with a setting up of a Palestinian Interim Self Governing Authority, leading to a permanent settlement based on UN resolutions 242 and 338. The implication, subtly suggested by the text, was that a state of Palestine would one day be set up alongside that of Israel.

Both sides exchanged letters recognising their right to exist but Hamas and other Palestinian factions, and also Israeli settler groups, refused to accept the conditions. What followed was a wave of suicide bombs on Israelis and the agreement was not fully implemented.

More talks took place at **Camp David** in 2000 but, despite detailed negotiations, there was no real progress with neither side willing to make radical concessions of territory and the meeting was followed by a renewal of the Intifada or Palestinian uprising.

In 2001 Bill Clinton was about to leave office and he set up more talks in Washington, Cairo and then **Taba** in Egypt. This time there was more flexibility on key issues, particularly on the idea of East Jerusalem becoming the capital of a Palestinian state, but the talks stalled.

After the failure of these talks and the resumption of violence, Saudi Arabia organised an Arab summit in **Beirut** in 2002 with the intention of bringing the entire dispute to a mutually agreeable end. It was proposed that Israel would withdraw to the borders of June 1967, a Palestinian state would be set up in the West bank, and Gaza and the refugee crisis would be resolved. As a mark of goodwill Arab countries would then recognise Israel. Many observers saw this as a significant breakthrough, but there was still the problem of negotiating the intricate details that had proved problematic in the previous talks.

The in 2003 came **"The Roadmap"**. This was a plan drawn up by the US, Russia, the European Union and the UN with Palestinian and Israeli consultation. Again it was short on detail but it did suggest how a settlement might be reached. George Bush told a conference of Arab leaders that he envisaged "a continuous territory that Palestinians can call home".

The plan was to be implemented in three stages and be complete by 2005. Firstly there was to be a dismantling of Israeli settlement outposts built since March 2001 and a staged withdrawal from the occupied territories. At the same time there would be an immediate cessation of Palestinian violence and a reform of its political institutions. Secondly there would be an international conference on the road map and the creation of an independent Palestinian state. Thirdly, Arab states would agree peace deals with Israel and final borders and the status of Jerusalem would be agreed upon.

Unfortunately the Roadmap has not been implemented, but it still remains acceptable by both sides as a fair and reasonable guideline, for future negotiations.

The Geneva Accord in 2003 was an informal agreement which reversed the proposals of the Roadmap, placing the treaty first, thus allowing security and peace to follow rather than the other way round but once again little progress was made. In his second presidential term US President George Bush invited delegates from all sides, including a dozen Arab countries, to a conference at the US Naval Academy at Annapolis, **Maryland,** and hopes were raised by Saudi Arabia and Syria's attendance, as they did not officially recognise Israel. The Palestinian group Hamas, however, which had been elected in the Gaza Strip, was not represented and it refused to honour any decision made by the others.

Barack Obama took office in 2009 and immediately tried to resume peace talks through his Middle East envoy George Mitchell. Israel's Prime Minister Benjamin Netanyahu was persuaded to agree to a ten month partial freeze on settlement construction in the West Bank, hailing his decision as "the first meaningful step towards peace" but the PLO's Mahmoud Abbas objected that the issue of Jerusalem was not mentioned and that if a guarantee of a Palestinian state was on the agenda it should be based on a return to the 1967 borders. Both sides did agree to meet in Washington in 2010 but negotiations predictably broke down, primarily over the two issues of settlements and borders.

In 2016 both Mr Netanyahu and Mr Abbas addressed the UN General Assembly and stated their key positions in unequivocal terms. It was clear that, despite years of initiatives and suggested compromises, there was still a monumental chasm between the opposing points of view.

Mr Abbas urged the Assembly to declare 2017 "the international year to end the Israeli occupation of our land and people" adding that "our hands remain outstretched for peace" but that Israel refuses to "abandon the mentality of hegemony, expansion and colonisation, choosing occupation over peace".

In reply, Mr Netanyahu blamed the Palestinian leader for "poisoning the future". He explained that Israel was ready to resume peace talks but rejected a freeze on Israeli settlement building as the issue had always been about "the existence of a Jewish state". He also rejected the 1967 borders as the basis for talks and denounced what he called Palestinian violence.

All of this makes depressing reading but in my opinion it is imperative that the deadlock be broken and I have faith that someday it will. This is not wishful thinking or blind naivety. I think a solution is possible, on the basis that violence is anathema to the human spirit and that there are historic, inspirational precedents for peace which can inform the present impasse.

I believe it is vital that both sides acknowledge that mistakes and atrocities have been committed and that neither side assumes the role of the permanent victim. We must have justice and transparency in any future dialogue and an open admission of realities, stripped of easy propaganda. Polarisation, ignoring facts, just ensures a festering and poisoning of differences.

There have been so many doom-laden predictions that if there is going to be a third world war, then the likely starting point will be in the Middle East, with Israel and Palestine as the focus. With JASTA appearing on the scene that possibility, in my opinion, could become much more likely and it is therefore imperative that a resumption of dialogue and negotiations be a priority.

Chapter Nine

JASTA AND THE NEW NATIONALISM

"If you believe you are a citizen of the world, you're a citizen of nowhere. You don't understand what the very word 'citizenship' means." UK Prime Minister Theresa May was addressing a Conservative party conference, aiming her remarks at rich people who allegedly align themselves with an international elite rather than with their own home grown society.

She was speaking just before Donald Trump became President of the US, persuading sixty one million Americans to vote for his brand of patriotic populism and promising them a "historic once-in-a lifetime-change". He also promised to deport illegal immigrants, build a wall on the Mexican border, imprison Hillary Clinton and "make America great again".

Welcome to the world of the new nationalism where patriotism is no longer a dirty word and the transnational elites, while not quite in freefall, are having to reassess their strategies for survival.

The US has a long tradition of challenging powerful elites and empires by supporting small nations in their struggles for independence. I doubt if President Trump is aware of it but he isn't the first US president to play the patriotic card. Woodrow Wilson took the Americans into the First World War and was instrumental in helping the states of Czechoslovakia, Hungary and Yugoslavia to gain national recognition as they emerged from the Hapsburg Empire, and the Russian Empire saw the Baltic states, Poland and Finland follow a similar path. It was General Eisenhower's refusal to back Great Britain and France in their attempt to occupy the Suez canal in 1956, that sealed the fate of their two empires.

The rise of this nationalism is not confined to just the US or the UK. In Russia Vladimir Putin has shifted the emphasis away from the international communist crusade with a newly found admiration for Russian history, Orthodox Christianity and a revival of Slavic traditions. He was possibly reacting to popular unrest from a frustrated middle class about high level corruption and uncontrolled immigration from other ethnic non Slavic minorities. He adopted a militaristic stance when Ukraine looked to have closer ties with the West. Much to the delight of the Russian populace he annexed Crimea and sent forces into eastern Ukraine, claiming he was there to protect the Russian minorities from "fascist groups". In effect he is rejecting and challenging the international liberal consensus that has dominated politics since the Second World War. This perhaps explains why he seems to recognize a soulmate in Donald Trump and other nationalist leaders.

He has a fellow supporter in Viktor Orban, the conservative Hungarian Prime Minister who embraced Trump's election by announcing that western civilization was now free from the confines of an ideology. "We are living in the days where what we call liberal non-democracy ends and we can return to real democracy. We can now call problems by their name and find solutions not derived from an ideology but based on pragmatic common sense. We are two days after the big bang (the US election) and still alive. What a wonderful world. This also shows that democracy is creative and innovative."

In China, Malaysia and Indonesia there are more strings of nationalism. The ruling communist party, aware of a slowing of economic growth, is busy promoting "The Chinese dream" to promote the country's revival. They still have an eye on international markets and they are members of global institutions but since the 1990s schoolchildren have been given lessons in patriotism; in fact in 2015 China's education minister criticized schools that still used textbooks promoting "western values". Like the Russians, they are also keen on re-examining their recent history, particularly the victory over Japan in the Second World War, and have introduced three new holidays commemorating massacres and the eventual Japanese surrender. When Japan countered in 2012, making territorial claims to islands in the East China Sea, there were riots: Japanese cars were destroyed, shops were looted and riot police were called out to defend their embassy in Beijing.

A similar story is being played out in Egypt where President Abdel-Fattah al-Sisi actively encourages patriotic feeling by reminding the public about Egypt's rich cultural heritage. He justifies the clamping down on the international Muslim brotherhood by emphasizing the benefits of order and stability which he sees as vital to the country's economic progress.

Further north, Turkey was doing everything it could to join the EU but that has now changed. Its president, Recep Tayyip Erdogan, has promised, like Trump and XI Jinping, to build "a new Turkey" lacing his speeches with anti-western, pro-Islamic messages. Sources inside Turkey blame this volte-face on the West's continuous interference in and criticism of the country's lack of press freedom and judicial independence. There are reports from the EU and the US that claim democratic freedoms are being eroded while Russia, on the other hand, has nothing but praise for Erdogan, with Putin hailing him as a "tough man". I think Putin admires Erdogan's refusal to bow to the politically correct values promoted by the international community and his advice to the EU to mind its own business.

He is yet another political leader who is rejecting western style liberalism by encouraging popular nationalism. He is in a strong position having won two general elections and helped the country to unprecedented economic growth.

In France the momentum is with Ms Marine Le Pen, a right wing presidential candidate and lawyer who is riding a tide of popular nationalism. Following the UK decision to leave the EU, she saw the Brexit result as proof that the EU was obsolete and decaying. "The UK has begun a movement that cannot be stopped," she said and sent her "warmest congratulations" to Boris Johnson and the Leave campaign, demanding that France should also be allowed its own referendum. She knows that this is unlikely to happen so has promised that if she is elected she will, within six months, hold an in/out referendum to decide the country's future. She then referred to the wide resurgence of what she called "patriotic" movements in other European countries. These include the anti-immigration and far right politician Geert Wilders who has called for a referendum on Dutch membership of the EU. He was echoed by the Danish People's Party's Kenneth Kristensen Berth who told the Danish media: "These European bureaucrats have been unusually adept at avoiding any possible confrontation with the massive popular opposition to the project. The British signal from Brexit cannot be overheard."

Another message of congratulation on the Brexit vote came from the far right Sweden democrats, the right wing German Alternative fur Deutschland party and The Golden Dawn nationalist party in Greece.

More anti-European sentiment, but this time more restrained, came from Italy's anti-establishment Five Star movement, which recently won 25% of the vote in a national election. The movement issued a strong critique of the EU demanding it should change or face extinction: "The leaving of the UK sets forth the failure of political communities facing austerity, and the egotism of the member states, incapable of being a community... We want a Europe which is a community and not a union of banks and lobbies."

There is, in my opinion, some very excitable rhetoric in these reactions and it has to be said that many of the above mentioned groups receive sympathy from even more extreme right wing movements. This I find disturbing. It is all very well to love your own country; this does not make you a racist or a xenophobe or a "deplorable", but national feeling can be manipulated and exploited, as fascist leaders in history have proved all too often. There is also the question of what brand of patriotism is being voted for. At the far extreme there is the dictatorial nationalism of Hitler, Mussolini, and a host of other murdering bullies. At the opposite end of that spectrum there is the benign form of Nationalism that celebrates unity, pride and an outward looking inclusiveness. It was Ronald Reagan, John Kennedy, Nelson Mandela, Winston Churchill and Mahatma Gandhi, among others, who championed this form of open and benevolent patriotism. Who can forget the defiant words of John Kennedy in front of the Berlin Wall in 1963, "Ich bin ein Berliner", thereby challenging the Soviet Union and assuring West Germany, and indeed the world, that America was their ally in upholding universal values of human rights and freedom.

Ronald Reagan wanted a country that "is not turned inward but outward – towards others" and, like Kennedy, he saw America as having a direct role to play in ensuring peace and prosperity for everyone, not just US citizens.

It is my hope that Donald Trump follows a similar path but he, by contrast, has vowed to put America first. He views the outer world with suspicion, threatening to retreat into a narrow form of isolationism. Election slogans were to build walls to keep immigrants out. He claims that the US is bankrolling the UN and NATO and that other countries are just freeloading, so he might just weaken the US's commitment to them both.

As outlined above he is not alone in embracing a pessimistic view that national interests are being eroded by global elitist ones.

The difference between his form of nationalism and Kennedy, Reagan, Churchill, Mandela and Gandhi's is, however, vast. The latter two when elected did not face a divided, bitter electorate and their grand visions were conciliatory and forward looking. They didn't have to work hard to convince people of their common values and aims.

A useful adjective to describe his form of nationalism is "ethnic". He made a direct appeal in his election campaign to the white working class poor who had seen their jobs cast aside and their protests unheard by the Washington elite.

He found a scapegoat in the masses of illegal immigrants, mainly from Mexico, but also the Muslims, who were to be barred from entry until their backgrounds were carefully checked. This kind of jingoistic drum-beating tends to produce intolerance and doubts about the motives and loyalties of minorities.

Where have we heard this kind of thing before? It is not too difficult to see parallels in the 1930s when mass unemployment, resentment at imposition of treaties and suspicion of minorities, particularly the Jews, led to the rise of extreme nationalism, fascism and the black nightmare of Adolf Hitler. I don't want to sound too alarmist but if "Jasta" does lead to a defensive reaction, with nation states feeling threatened by legal claims for compensation, and Donald Trump lives up to his aggressive inward-looking rhetoric, then I feel the world is on a dangerous path to some form of calamity.

If more countries retreat behind their barricades, global problems including poverty and refugee crises will necessarily become harder to solve. Three African nations left the ICC recently, the World Trade Organization is looking nervously over its shoulder at Trump's talk of tariffs and in Europe there is a worry that NATO will lose its principal paymaster and encourage the expansionist dreams of Vladimir Putin on its eastern borders. America has turned its back on the world before, after the First World War, and the consequences were appalling. Disengaging from the international scene will not keep America safe for very long and it is my hope that Mr Trump can remember the more visionary example of his predecessors and look out onto the world and not into a narrowing, excluding form of nationalism.

Chapter Ten

UNITED NATIONS, NATO, EUROPEAN UNION AND THE CHANGING WORLD ORDER

In late 2016 it became clear even to the liberal elites of the West that a new world order was beginning to take shape. The election of Donald Trump, the expansionist policies of Vladimir Putin, the continuing conflict in Syria, the shaking foundations of the EU and the onward march of China as a rival to the US economy were all signals that the road ahead was changing and that international confusion could see a retreat into defensive isolationism and frantic alliances as nations sought to protect themselves, as they did during the years leading up to the two world wars.

I have argued throughout that in a period of dramatic shifts in political templates it is paramount that clear thinking prevails. That is why I have stressed that JASTA could be a destabilising factor in increasing the tension in an already uncertain world.

I wish I could also argue that the UN could provide just that stabilising influence and reassurance but I can't.

Just after the Second World War the UN announced its noble aims through its magnificent charter but it has hardly changed in structure at all. It is now an extended organisation with myriad associated agencies, some accountable, some not. It has struggled to deal with new threats such as international terrorism and global diseases, and universal agreements have been hobbled by competing national interests as veto after veto by individual countries prevents any resolute action.

The chief players in the powerful Security Council are the same five that were first there in 1945: the US, Russia, China, Britain and France. Each one has a veto and can induce near paralysis on the other four when it comes to reaching a crucial decision. Since 1945 the US has vetoed 14 draft resolutions, particularly the ones relating to the Israeli-Palestinian conflict, and Russia has vetoed 11, mainly involving its allies in the Middle East such as Syria. Inevitably there is resentment from the other187 member states who feel marginalised from the primary business of international security. These countries are of course represented in the General Assembly, but that body cannot pass binding resolutions, only non-binding ones. Countries which should really be on the permanent Security Council would include, in my opinion, at least one from each continent, but it looks like the "big five" have no desire to let them in.

The apparent impotence of the Security Council was highlighted recently in the case of Ukraine, which has become a super power testing ground between Russia and the West, or NATO, with both parties in the conflict ignoring or just vetoing any potential binding resolutions. It is the same story in Syria with Russian support for President Bashar al-Assad preventing any UN interference or influence on the outcome of the war.

It is strategies like these that prevent any meaningful action and it is hard for the UN, despite its well-meaning objective, not to be seen as an expensive talking shop for international elites. Of course it undertakes immensely valuable humanitarian initiatives but one of its primary principles was its mandate to protect civilians when their own states were powerless to do so and in this it has been virtually toothless because there is no machinery for a conflict. In 1993, for example, the UN had declared the area around Srebrenica in Bosnia a safe haven, but it was unable to prevent the massacre of 8000 Muslim men and boys in July 1995 by government militias.

It is still an influential body but a period of profound change usually brings along its twin, uncertainty, and when international organisations act as if they are governments and are seen to be remote, ineffectual and unaccountable, then it is not surprising that there is a grassroots reaction and, in some cases, a renewal of nationalism as a necessary balancing factor. Quite often these bodies, such as the UN and the EU, grow rambling bureaucracies. The UN has fifteen autonomous agencies, eleven semi-autonomous ones and numerous other associated add-ons. Trying to coordinate these branches is immensely difficult as there is no central body with the capability of overseeing them.

To be fair the UN is very conscious of this problem and has tried to introduce transparency and accountability. As far as I know public opinion has never called for the abolition of the UN but it has repeatedly called out for reform. Having worked as Director General at WIPO, I am fully aware of this need for an analysis of recurring problems, particularly in funding and I would add that so called 'whistle-blowers', particularly of late, need official, institutional and credible protection.

This is an area where real reform could make a difference. Most UN agencies are financially dependent on mandatory contributions from member states. Agency budgets are then decided and each member's government pays a percentage of the total, determined by highly complicated calculations and intensive private bargaining, or what could loosely be called "haggling".

It is also common for entitlement programmes that are regularly funded to underperform as there is very little in the way of accountability, whereas agencies funded by voluntary contributions often perform more efficiently. UNICEF, the world food programme, for example, and others, have tended to be far more cost conscious and productive largely because, if they are perceived to be underperforming, the contributing funders will begin to look elsewhere to donate their money. To me this is just good business practice and voluntary funding would help the UN enormously. I would recommend, within reason because voluntary contributions can be unpredictable, that UN agencies should move from assessed or mandatory contributions to voluntary ones as quickly as possible. This would have two positive effects. Firstly it would make them instantly accountable and probably more efficient and secondly it would mollify public opinion that the money, especially from the larger contributors, was being spent wisely.

Despite its shortcomings, I still feel that the UN has a vital part to play in harmonising international relations and in providing aid to disaster stricken areas and countries. In that sense it can have a positive influence, but as a body which can act as a restraint on aggression or conflict, it is at the moment handicapped inter alia by the veto system.

If JASTA does indeed have a destabilising influence on world affairs, with sovereign states facing legal challenges and retreating into nationalism, then NATO, not just the UN, could come under serious international pressure.

It has been argued that it is NATO that has guaranteed the peace of the post Second World War, acting as a deterrent to aggression from the Soviet Union throughout the following cold one. When that "war" ended there were obvious calls for the alliance to be disbanded as an expensive irrelevance with doubtful objectives, but

Russia's expansionist moves in Crimea in 2014, which marked the first forcible annexation of territory in Europe since 1945, meant that NATO was back in business.

Critics are quick to point out that President Trump has complained openly about NATO's weaknesses and shortcomings while at the same time making favourable comments about Putin. It is possible, however, that his intent might be to strengthen NATO by persuading member countries to fulfil their financial obligations for the sake of their own security. He is just repeating calls from like minded US officials that have gone on for decades. He sees an alliance of strong national governments signing up to a mutual defence treaty as a major factor in discouraging aggression. It should be remembered that within days of Ronald Reagan's election in an atmosphere similar to that of Trump's, and Jimmy Carter's disappearance from the political scene, Iran surrendered its American hostages within a very short time. Possibly it might have known what was coming if it hadn't.

President Trump is an astute and forceful businessman who sees politics in terms of deals and compromises and I'm sure his dynamism and sincere patriotism will be tempered by sound counsel from his advisors.

Unlike the EU which has voiced desires to form its equivalent to NATO and which assumes central control and a dilution of national sovereignty, NATO is a combination of vigorous states with mutually agreed objectives. Article 5, which guarantees the security of each member, is the glue that binds it all together and it is exactly the kind of organisation that America feels it can support. Given the fractious nature of the EU and even the growing concern about its survival, it would be difficult to see how it could ever match the resolve and unity of purpose of NATO in forming a defensive alliance.

In addition, it could be that NATO is about to assume a global rather than a North Atlantic role. Jose Maria Aznar, the former Spanish Prime Minister, has recently suggested admitting new members, shifting the emphasis more towards the African and Asian land masses, a move that could have profound consequences for those countries feeling nervous about JASTA.

For the EU politicians in Brussels, however, the break-up of the organisation is unthinkable, just as the break-up of the Hapsburg Empire in 1914, the British one after the Second World War and the Soviet Union in 1990 were. No one could have foreseen just how quickly these monolithic structures would disintegrate and it could be that within a short time the EU itself will collapse before an astonished world. The rise of nationalist parties in France, Germany, Italy, Austria, Hungary, Poland, Sweden, The Netherlands and Britain is a confirmation of an acute distrust of an "empire" completely out of touch with its ethnic roots, and the frustration with centralised power in the hands of unelected and unaccountable political elites.

The catastrophe of the eclipse of the Hapsburg Empire in particular has worrying parallels with the present day. It too, like the EU, tried to unify a diverse group of culturally and linguistically linked countries into a governable whole and then found that a pistol shot from a Serbian nationalist gun could begin the process of destruction.

I do appreciate that the EU was formed, like the UN, on ideals of peace, freedom and prosperity for all, but the appalling rates of unemployment in the Mediterranean countries, the lack of sovereign independence, the confusion over immigration, the over regulation of businesses, the protection of its borders and the sluggish economic growth rate, are indications of a lack of purpose and confidence. I also appreciate that the principal aim of the EU was to prevent the rise of extreme nationalism which led to the Second World War, that authoritarianism, either of the left or the right would never again dominate the political scene. I think these ideals were sincere and honourable, as were those of the other global institutions that followed. The World Bank, the International Monetary Fund and of course the UN were formed to help prevent conflict and harmonise the world economy. Now the viability of these institutions is being questioned, mainly from the forces of the right and nationalist sympathisers. In Europe, there has been a hardening of nationalism which could morph into extreme nationalism, or even fascism, because of the threat posed by JASTA. All of which is almost a mirror image of the conditions that led to the two world wars of the twentieth century.

If liberal democracy is to survive, therefore, it has to look to the causes of its demise and unpopularity. It has to admit to itself that, though it guarantees freedom of speech and accountability from its elected governments, it also has to address the inequalities that it promotes. The huge profits of the global giants of the digital age such as Amazon and Google and other international companies can lead to resentment from the poor and the questioning of capitalism itself. It also has to address the genuine fears of sensible majorities about uncontrolled immigration and the centralisation of power in the hands of a distanced elite. At the same time, it has also got to be more forthright in the defence of its record. There are huge economic woes but globalisation has helped to eradicate severe poverty in many parts of the world and democracy, despite its failures, is still the only real guarantee of freedom from dictators and autocrats.

It could also be that the revolt against the global giants stems from a subconscious awareness among sections of the populace that the old saying of "small is beautiful" has a measure of truth in it. There is a school of thought that the reason that Europe became a dominant, creative and wealthy continent was not because it was one vast centralised monolith, like the current EU, but because it was a collection of small independent countries in direct competition with each other. These countries experimented with different forms of government, encouraged innovation and allowed businesses to expand by lowering taxes. In the 1700s Britain, for example, decided to lower its taxes considerably and Dutch businessmen saw their chance. They emigrated, bringing with them their financial nous and technological expertise, thereby highlighting the advantages of liberty and free movement. Others weren't so fortunate. If you had a brilliant idea the chances are you would be held captive so that the neighbours couldn't steal it, which was what happened to an eighteenth century alchemist in Saxony called Johann Friedrich Bottger, who claimed he had discovered the secret of making gold. The prince imprisoned him in a castle in case other countries lured him away to profit from his discoveries. It turned out that Bottger couldn't make gold but he did discover how to make world class porcelain, much to the delight of the Prince and his treasury.

If small was beautiful, innovative and productive, large was the exact opposite. China was a monolithic state governed from the centre, a vast empire with a uniform tax system and very little free movement of people. With virtually no neighbours to compete with, a static economy and minimal experimentation, it was no wonder that it fell behind the dynamic European model. Now the EU, with its sprawling bureaucracy, uniform tax demands and single currency obsession is in danger of becoming an example of an over regulated state just like China was in the seventeenth century. It is telling innovative thinkers that government rules and regulations, and overall harmonisation must come first; the precise opposite of what was encouraged in previous ages in Europe.

So the ballot boxes in the liberal democracies are currently sending a clear message to their political representatives. They are demanding less centralisation of power, more awareness of the negative side effects of globalisation in terms of loss of jobs and local investment, a return to national sovereignty and a curbing of rules and regulations that stifle innovation.

I believe this process could be of great benefit to the world economy in stimulating growth and restoring national pride with a consequent increase in productivity and self-confidence. The obvious worry, however, is that this nationalism could easily develop into an extreme form where competition becomes aggressive, self-seeking and ruthless and, as in the case of Nazi Germany, the democratic process becomes bypassed and the rule of law is abandoned.

That is why I believe that JASTA could have such an unsettling influence on global harmony. By its implied threat to national governments, it could lead to an intensified form of nationalism and the formation of new, less stable alliances, as in 1914 and 1939. In other words, another world war.

Chapter Eleven

GLOBALISATION AND FREE TRADE

"We're going to make America great again!" was Donald Trump's rallying cry to the depressed rust belts of the mid-west, where unemployment and frustration at being ignored by the Washington elites led to mass resentment among the blue collar workers who had seen their jobs outsourced abroad. Cheap imports and illegal immigrant workers had left vast areas of poverty, decaying industries and an angry working class. While Hillary Clinton dismissed these people as "deplorables", Trump hailed them as the true, forgotten Americans, promising that if he became president he would protect their jobs and revive their industries by opposing free trade and imposing tariffs on imports.

To my mind this is economic nationalism and an as yet undeclared war on free trade or globalisation, which in turn could have disastrous consequences leading to a worldwide recession.

Since 1945 the international economic order has been founded on the principles of free trade and integration and a move to isolationism or protectionism could have a devastating effect on the entire structure. It should be remembered that it was the depressions of the 1920s and 30s that coincided with the rise of fascism in Europe and the road to the Second World War.

At that time a collapse of the American GDP ushered in the Smoot-Hawley Tariff Act which had catastrophic consequences on world trade. It wasn't until 1944 that the General Agreement on Tariffs and Trade (GATT) committed allied governments to lower tariffs.

When more agreements followed, world trade tripled during the 1980s and 90s but the economic crisis in 2008 resulted in weak growth and stagnant industries. Mr Trump blamed free trade and outsourcing for the resulting decline in living standards and announced that if he were to be elected he would immediately impose import tariffs on China to cut the American trade deficit. He added that he would also cancel the climate agreement that President Obama had signed with President Xi Jinping in September 2016.

It is widely accepted that this would not only alienate a potential trading giant, the world's second largest economy, but would also have a ripple effect on related economies in the wider world. It is also accepted that free trade is a win-win situation for both parties by allowing them to specialise in certain products that are non-competitive and which complement each other.

In the short term there might be gains for America by imposing tariffs, as unemployment falls and inward investment boosts growth, but in the long term economic nationalism is a dead end, as the country's exports will be undercut by foreign prices and their protected industries become inefficient.

The Chinese reaction to Mr Trump's threats has been surprisingly muted. The Communist Party's People's Daily newspaper announced in a recent editorial that the trade relationship between the world's two largest economies was so important that any breakdown in ties could result in global "disaster".

In another development it seems that Mr Trump's bombastic rhetoric of the election campaign is softening. Just as he is no longer promising to have Hillary Clinton "jailed", he is no longer casting China as the villain, out to destroy the American economy. The paper noted that the first exchanges between President Xi and Mr Trump were cooperative and productive: "The two leaders had a good chat, a positive atmosphere and reached important consensus." The optimism in the report might be a reflection that Mr Trump, as a businessman, is aware that if he wants to bring back jobs and promote growth at home, he has to take a pragmatic approach to free trade and international engagement. These initial stages of engagement might include fake "kabuki" negotiations which would reassure his root supporters at home that he is taking a hard line, but there is some evidence that Chinese opinion would view these as cosmetic. They know that if he wants to "Make America great again" he cannot retreat into protectionism.

They also seem to sense that in some way the two men recognise that they have parallel ambitions for their countries. Not long after he became President in 2012, Xi Jinping announced that China was now on a road to a "Great Revival", with an emphasis on patriotic enthusiasm leading to huge economic renaissance and national confidence. It couldn't be closer to that of "The American Dream" which Mr Trump is convinced he can realise.

The "Great Revival", however, might not look so great in about twenty years' time when other problems appear. China has two huge structural concerns, like many other "developed" countries, particularly in Europe, but also in Russia and Japan. It has an aging, male dominated population, the biggest demographic imbalance in history. This was a direct result of the self-inflicted policy of the communist "one baby" policy which ensured mass state-inflicted abortions. The country is also so lacking in crucial resources that it recently signed a deal to lease 5% of Ukraine, an area about the size of Belgium, to grow its own crops. This isn't surprising as only 9% of its huge area is fit for farming and it consumes 20% of the world's food.

These exchanges with the Chinese government indicate that there are some signs that Mr Trump is listening to "wise men" and that he is acknowledging his limited experience in global matters.

It will be fascinating to see how the newly elected President Trump relates to Vladimir Putin, given the initial complimentary remarks of both men towards each other. Whether Trump is able to restrain Putin on any further challenges to eastern European borders remains to be seen. I believe that Mr Trump's appreciative overtures to Putin will be welcomed, but his resolve will be tested by repeated Russian military pressure on the Ukraine and the Baltic borders. The war in Syria looks to be unwinnable but it could be that a combined Russian/American diplomatic initiative promoting the division of the country into self-governing regions, as achieved twenty years ago in the dissolving of Yugoslavia, might lead to a temporary peace and provide some form of escape route for Bashar al-Assad.

Isis does seem to believe that it is on a divinely ordained mission to confront and annihilate the Kufars or infidels by luring then into Syria for an apocalyptic battle. According to its online propaganda magazine "Dabiq", this battle will end in a defeat for the crusader forces in Dabiq itself, near the northern city of Aleppo. This prophecy is perhaps why President Obama didn't want to enter the narrative and restricted the US engagement to limited airstrikes.

If Mr Trump goes ahead with his promise of bombing Isis I fear that it might prove counterproductive by attracting more support from young firebrands outraged by what they see as another "invasion", similar to the one in Iraq. This in turn could lead to bordering countries forming defensive alliances with the super powers, then having to engage by taking sides and possibly opposing one another, just as they did before the outbreak of the First World War.

A more likely outcome in my opinion is that as Isis is pushed out of Syria and Iraq it will change its strategy and concentrate on spectacular attacks in European cities. What it is trying to do is to provoke a reaction against Muslims worldwide and it doesn't care what depths of brutality are necessary to achieve that aim.

The picture is further complicated by the antagonism between Sunni and Shia Muslims. There is sometimes a misconception that the entire Islamic world is at war with western values but the reality is that thousands of Muslims have been killed by terrorist atrocities. There were several dozen innocent Muslims killed during the 9/11 attacks, including people in their late 60s and a couple with an unborn child. Most of them were stockbrokers or restaurant workers and many were immigrants from a wide variety of countries, and more than thirty Muslim children were left orphaned after the attack. The world's 1.6 billion Muslims are peaceable and well intentioned and it is an extremist minority which is driving the violence and challenging the values of Western democracy.

In my view it will be ideas and values that will win these conflicts, rather than endless, reciprocal violence. The extremists can terrorise and kill as much as they want but they cannot ever conquer the human spirit and its instinctive desire for freedom of speech, tolerance and human rights.

Chapter Twelve

JASTA AND THE FIRST WORLD WAR

It was a pistol shot that reverberated through history. When Gavrilo Princip, a young Serbian nationalist, put two bullets into the bodies of Archduke Ferdinand of Austria-Hungary and his wife the Duchess Sophie on June 28th, 1914 the world went into a tailspin. He was unapologetic: "I am a Yugoslav nationalist, aiming for the unification of all Yugoslavs, and I do not care what form of State, but it must be free from Austria." What followed with their deaths, was the First World War and indirectly the second one. Princip wasn't the primary cause – there were other multiple factors in play.

I have no problem with **patriotism**. Love of one's native land is a fine thing and I disagree with the Englishman Samuel Johnson who claimed that nationalism was "the last refuge of the scoundrel". After all, if we can't love our own country how can we possible appreciate or love someone else's? I think what Johnson was referring to was an extreme form of nationalism. This of course reached its apogee in Germany when the Third Reich under Adolf Hitler preached its own form of National Socialism.

We can go back centuries to examine this idea but an obvious starting point would be the origins of the First World War (1914-

1918). Many books have already been written on this topic and I don't want to start analysing in too much detail about the variety of causes. To a neutral bystander, the years leading up to the outbreak were a time of calm, peace and prosperity, but there was a disturbing undercurrent of opinion that with huge standing armies being raised and factories belching out masses of rifles, ships and ammunition one day there really would be a war. In addition there was a highly complex mixture of political, social and economic factors that politicians either preferred to ignore or just couldn't handle.

Until the summer of 1914, however, the chimerical dance of peace and diplomacy held sway.

The Archduke Franz Ferdinand of Austria-Hungary, a quarrelsome, arrogant man, had deepened his unpopularity at home by marrying a mere Countess. Sophie Chotek was far beneath him on the social scale and royal protocol prevented her from becoming an archduchess or imperial highness. She was forbidden to sit side by side with him on social occasions and her children could never assume their place in the succession. The only time she could officially accompany him was when he was inspecting troops. This was the one time where his role as a Field Marshall of the army trumped his royal title. Ferdinand decided that a suitable way of celebrating their wedding anniversary on the 28th June 1914 was by inspecting his army in nearby Bosnia. This was a highly dangerous thing to do but, with typical obstinacy, he ignored advice from his staff and set off with his wife.

At the time Bosnia and its province, Hercegovina, were seething hotbeds of revolt. Formerly part of Turkey it had been administered by Austria-Hungary since 1878 and then annexed in 1908. Now there was simmering resentment at being separated from what the Bosnians saw as their national state of Serbia. Their conquests of neighbouring territories had alarmed the Austrians and the military governor declared a state of emergency, dissolving Parliament, shutting down schools and suspending the justice system. The Austrian went further and announced that military manoeuvres would take place in Sarajevo. If this was not inflammatory enough, the Archduke insisted that he and the duchess would be there in person to inspect the troops.

Princip, a seventeen year old grammar schoolboy and son of a postal worker, saw his chance. He and five of his friends had been given some basic weapons and the blessing of a secret nationalist society called Apis. What followed was a bungling farce. When the Archduke's open car came into view one of the boys threw a bomb but it bounced off and rolled under a following car, exploding and injuring an army officer. Another had a pang of conscience and went home and another struggled to draw his gun. Frustrated and probably embarrassed they slunk into a nearby café. The bomb had enraged the Archduke: "So this is how you welcome guests, with bombs!" and he demanded that his driver head straight out of Sarajevo. On the way he took a wrong turning and stopped the car before trying to reverse. Amazingly he was right outside the café where the assassins had gathered and Princip leapt from his seat, mounted the car's running board and fired at both the archduke and his wife. Sophie was hit on her right side and died on the way to a hospital from loss of blood, Ferdinand was hit in his jugular vein, the bullet coming to rest against his spine and he died shortly after his wife.

Princip knew that he was a doomed man and tried to shoot himself at the scene but his pistol was knocked out of his hand and he was rushed to a police station before a mob could close in and kill him. He later tried to poison himself with cyanide but failed again. He was young enough to escape the death penalty and died later in Theresienstadt prison in Austria of tuberculosis of the bone in

1918, but earlier he had been examined by a psychiatrist. Had he any regrets about being the man who had caused a whole continent to destroy itself, thereby wiping out generations of young men like himself? His answer was that if he hadn't done it someone else would have and that war was inevitable.

How would the rulers of Austria-Hungary respond to this outrage? Unwilling to seem weak and ineffective they decided to take a strong line but they took their time. They wanted proof that the Serbian Government had had a hand in the assassination. They never got it. In the meantime they had turned to their German ally for help and on the 5th July they got it. The Emperor Wilhelm II, backed by his Chancellor Bethmann Hollweg, urged the Austrians to threaten Serbia with a full scale invasion. They also promised support if Russia backed the Serbians. There is doubt among historians that this grandstanding was a deliberate attempt to escalate a war. Tensions had been high in the past between the great empires but diplomacy had always won through in the end and it is probable that these initiatives and threats were mere sabre rattling, hollow threats to appease their various populations and not to be taken too seriously.

There is another school of thought, however, that this was precisely the time when Germany saw its chance to expand its empire. Throughout the previous twenty or thirty years it had been matching Great Britain in a frantic arms race. Both these countries were the leading industrial and economic powers of the first rank, closely followed by the United States, and neither could afford to lag behind the other in military strength, even though the thought of war was a side issue. Building huge navies was just a precautionary measure. There were generals on either side, though, who were always thinking the unthinkable and prepared to voice their views. Military opinion in Germany could argue that war was inevitable and that the present moment was the time to seize the initiative. Austria-Hungary and Russia were struggling to keep pace with Germany in terms of manpower and Italy wasn't even in the race. The Turkish Ottoman Empire, never having kept up with modernization and economic change was in decline and as "the sick man of Europe" would see the end of its empire by 1918. The British would be horrified at the thought of a continental war and anyway their eyes were on their overseas empire, especially in the Far East. Any quarrel that involved Russia could see their vital trade link through the Suez Canal threatened.

If the surrounding empires were relatively weak in themselves, however, they were formidable in their combined alliances and it was understandable that Germany felt itself surrounded and threatened. If war did come it would probably have to fight on two fronts, against its traditional enemy France in the west and the ally of Serbia, Russia, in the east. This would be suicidal so the intelligent thing to do was to defeat France first and then turn towards Russia. It knew that if war was declared it could mobilise its vast army very quickly indeed and deal with France. It also knew that it would take weeks, even months, for the Russians to gather their forces. The Russian railway system was primitive in the extreme and it would take a monumental effort to transport its armies to the front line. As well as this, rumblings of a communist revolution had diverted the government's attention away from full mobilisation. By the time they got their troops into position Germany would have dealt with France and be ready to face them on the eastern front.

The point I am making is that Princip was a fervent **nationalist** and this alone in his eyes justified the murder. It is my conviction that this nationalism was the root cause of the conflict and that imperialism, militarism, a lack of diplomatic common sense and dialogue and communication were important but only secondary factors.

Leaping ahead into the twenty first century, it is my further belief that JASTA, because of its threat to sovereignty, could indirectly reignite the fires of nationalism and force groups of countries into defensive alliances, similar to the situation in 1914. We have learned from history that excessive nationalism, particularly in the case of Hitler or Mussolini, can rouse latent aggressive and primitive emotions. A sense of righteousness, a sense of destiny, a sense that racial superiority is a God given fact and that expansion into foreign territory is therefore justified, leads to hideous barbarities and an inevitable suspension of civilised values. The dogs of war are unleashed. It is my aim in this book to make sure that these dogs stay under control on a secure lead and harm no one.

But what made Gavrilo Princip pull the trigger? What were the undercurrents of his rage? In 1871 Germany was the dominant country in Europe when it defeated France under the leadership of Chancellor Bismarck. Though the victor over France, it was never as powerful as the three great empires on its flanks, the Russians, the Austrians and the Turks. What Germany did was to encourage the smaller nations, such as Poland and Serbia, to voice their **nationalist** feelings and demand independence. It also had a new young leader, Kaiser Wilhelm II, who was casting envious eyes at the mighty British empire, then at its zenith. The British industrial output and its overseas colonies ensured vast wealth and its guardian was the formidable Royal Navy. Germany began a process of catching up, militarising, and Europe looked on with alarm. After Bismarck's victory in 1871 it had annexed the territories of Alsace and Lorraine from France. Alliances began to form. If Germany was a growing threat it was only sensible for France to ally itself with Russia, completing a potential "encirclement" of Germany. This was a blow to Bismarck but his attention turned south. He knew that the Turkish Empire was weakening and that his own ally, Austria, had its eyes on expansion into the Balkans, but so did Russia.

In strategic terms, and in relation to the developed world, Russia was virtually landlocked and its vital port of entry to Europe and beyond for its exports was the Dardanelles Strait through the Black Sea and into the Mediterranean. Russia knew that Turkey could throttle this gateway at will and had in fact done so temporarily in 1911 during the Italian War. The result had been an economic disaster with vast piles of Russian grain left rotting and unsold in Crimean harbours. Conscious of Russian pressure to keep the straits open, Turkey turned to Germany for protection.

In 1894 France and Russia had formed an alliance, a mutual assurance that if either of them were attacked the other would come to its aid. It was at this point that the huge German navy presented itself to the world. The British thought they had no option but to respond and an arms race was the outcome. They not only outpaced the Germans by doubling their fleet, they also formed defence accommodations with the French and Russians. Already it seemed as if the battle lines for a massive European war were being drawn.

The one country that was trying to remain neutral by not entering into any alliances was Great Britain. It had had longstanding wars with France over the centuries and the recent memory of Napoleon's threat to invade was still in living memory. Mothers would tell their children that if they didn't behave and go to sleep "Boney" would creep into their bedrooms at night and kidnap them! Great Britain's eyes were on its overseas empire and it was occupied in protecting it with its navy. Certainly a war with Germany was unthinkable. Their royal families were related, they were emerging as a stable country with democratic advances and their cultural achievements, including Goethe and Beethoven, were second to none.

It was now that **nationalism** began to pour drops of oil onto a smoking fire. As previously mentioned, in 1908 Austria-Hungary annexed the Balkan provinces of Herzegovina and Bosnia, arguing that they had been given the right to administer them temporarily by the Congress of Berlin. Officially these provinces lay under the jurisdiction of the Turks. The Russians accepted the annexation mainly because it saw that France had no interest in the matter and was unlikely to support it. The Serbs, together with the Bosnians and Slavs, who now found themselves under Austrian "protection" demanded their freedom. The visit of Archduke Franz Ferdinand to Sarajevo, the capital of Bosnia, was a colonial insult too far. Enter Gavrilo Princip with his revolver.

The rest, as they say, is history. The assassinated Archduke had not been a popular figure but the Austrians demanded that the Serbian government bring the culprits to justice, expecting that nothing would happen and thus they would have a pretext for launching an invasion. In the background was Germany, delighted with what had just happened. When Princip had voiced that a war was inevitable he was only stating the obvious. In retrospect it does seem that Germany was ready for a fight. A war-happy diplomat in the Austro-Hungarian Foreign Ministry announced that the murder of the Archduke was "a gift from Mars". Now the Hapsburg Empire would be great again. With Germany as its powerful ally the Russians could be faced down and the weakening Turkish Empire could be taken over. It all depended on the Austrians forcing the Serbs into war, thereby bringing their ally Russia to defend them. Despite the fiery rhetoric from their Foreign Minister, the Austrians were very wary of rousing the mighty Russian bear but their big brother Germany had other ideas, demanding that Austria issue an ultimatum to the Serbs which they knew could not be met.

The Austrian played for time, making excuse after excuse for delaying, but once the Germans started putting diplomatic pressure on them they sent the ultimatum. This virtually guaranteed the loss of Serbian independence. The Serbs, facing humiliation, had no choice but to refuse and on 28th July war was declared. In many ways Austria's declaration of war was a gigantic bluff, a diplomatic manoeuvre. Its armies were in a poor state of preparation and it was gambling on the hope that Russia would not honour its alliance with Serbia. It also knew that if it mobilised its armies against Serbia it couldn't possible mobilise against the Russians as well.

How would the Russians respond? Initially the Russian Tsar was in a state of denial and couldn't believe that the Austrians were serious. Even the German ambassador, when handing over the declaration of war, did so in tears. The problem for the Russians was that if Germany and Austro-Hungary swept south through the Balkans, they would control Constantinople, now Istanbul, and effectively threaten its access to the wider world. The narrow straits that separated Europe from Asia were Russia's jugular vein, its economic pipeline.

Sensing the scale of the crisis, the German Emperor began to have second thoughts, even sending diplomatic telegrams to the Russians, but his generals were adamant that there should be no going back. They were confident that their own superior rail network could bring hundreds of thousands of troops to the front line weeks before the Russians thereby gaining a massive strategic and game changing advantage.

The Russians realised that if they mobilised against Austria-Hungary they would be unable to defend themselves against Germany and their only face-saving choice to keep pace with the diplomatic charade was to order a huge general mobilisation. This was by no means an aggressive step. They were reluctant to go to war and their tactics were aimed at survival rather than conquest.

They wanted to show that in the international game of bluff and counter bluff they could match the Austrians. In fact they were secretly hoping that someone would have the common sense to call an international conference to defuse the situation. Sadly there was no one with the leadership or perception to bring the various alliances to the negotiating table. On 30th July Russia began the process of amassing its huge reserves of manpower into a fighting force and the troop trains began to rattle into place. Once they began their journeys to the front lines they were virtually impossible to stop.

The Germans knew this only too well and had already had experience of taking the initiative in 1870 by getting their thousands of soldiers into line well before the French could organise themselves properly. Speed was of the essence and railways won wars; it took the Germans only six weeks to surround the French, advance on Paris and win the war. Their Generals were itching to repeat the strategy and were overjoyed when general mobilisation was declared in Russia on 31st July. This meant that they could be seen as responding to aggression, that their own mobilisation was a defensive measure. The final act was for the German ambassador in Moscow to request an end to Russian mobilisation within twelve hours, a hollow act if ever there was one, and when this was refused, war was declared on 1st August. Two days later war was declared against France. The Germans were aware that if they faced war on two fronts they would lose and that they had to strike quickly, as in 1870.

They had already planned that it would be France and it was a former Chief of Staff who had masterminded it. Alfred von Schlieffen, though now dead, argued that the war could be won in the west by sidestepping the heavily fortified border with France and racing through the flat plains of Belgium. The French armies would be encircled and the war would be over in a few short weeks. But there was a problem. Belgium was a neutral power; its neutrality guaranteed by Great Britain and Germany. On 2nd August Germany demanded free access for its armies. The Belgians refused and the ever alert Winston Churchill, First Lord of the Admiralty, immediately ordered the British Royal Navy to action stations.

At this stage Great Britain had been trying very hard to keep out of the gathering storm, referring to the whole scenario as a "Balkan Quarrel" but it felt duty bound to honour its agreement with Belgium and declared war, reluctantly, on Germany. Meanwhile the Austrians were dithering, probably horrified at the appalling nightmare they had accidentally created. Goaded on by Germany they eventually declared war against Russia on 6th August and invaded Serbia on the 11th. Within two months they were in embarrassing retreat and the Serbs swept into southern Hungary. The finale to the outbreak came when Great Britain and France declared war against Austria-Hungary on the 10th August, the Turks announced an alliance with Germany on the same day and Japan declared war against Germany on the 23rd August.

The tragedy was that no one had any idea of the scale of carnage that was to follow. Cheering crowds, bunches of flowers and fresh faced young men flooded into recruitment centres and dreamed of exciting times with their friends. There was the assumption that it would all be over by Christmas and everyone would have a break from dull domesticity or the boring job. Both sides thought that God was on their side and their cause was just. The generals in particular basked in the thought that after the war their statues would adorn the various capital cities and that glory was theirs. Every nation had the feeling that they were on the defensive and that the best way forward was to seize the initiative and invade their neighbour. The only people who lowered their eyes and shook their heads were the hard faced bankers and economists who quite understandably worried about who was going to pay the bills. Interruption of foreign trade would hit everyone and unemployment and bankruptcy were forecast. When the Hungarian Foreign Minister was asked how long the war could be financed he replied "three weeks". In fact there was only enough money for three weeks, though it took longer than anticipated for the full effects to come through. In 1917 Russia sued for peace having undergone a Bolshevik revolution, and by 1918 almost the whole of Germany was facing starvation. In addition there was also one British politician, the Foreign Secretary, Sir Edward Grey, who couldn't share in the general euphoria. His prediction that "the lights are going out all over Europe. We shall not see them lit again in our lifetime" was deadly accurate.

"Those who don't know their history are condemned to repeat it." It wasn't Winston Churchill who coined this phrase but he certainly made use of it to warn Europe and the rest of the world about the advancing nightmare of Adolf Hitler and his brutal brand of National Socialism or Nazism. His critics thought Churchill was exaggerating. Surely Hitler couldn't be serious in threatening genocide and total war? Then as now there was complacency and lack of resolve in facing a direct threat to peace. It wasn't until the eve of war in 1939 that the nightmare became daytime reality.

Chapter Thirteen

WORLD WAR. THE INTERIM BETWEEN THE FIRST WORLD WAR AND THE SECOND

The guns stopped at 11.00 a.m. on 11th November 1918. Minutes after the ceasefire a German junior officer approached the American lines to tell them that the war was over and that they could have the house that he and his men had just vacated. Unaware of the armistice the Americans shot him dead. He was one of the last casualties of the war.

Millions, whole generations of young men, had been wiped out and the political map of the world was transformed. The relative peace of the 19th century was just a fading memory and faith in the strength of liberal values and the capitalist system was shaken. All across Europe families mourned for their lost sons, brothers and fathers. Hatred between nations persisted and one Austrian corporal became incensed at what he saw as a "stab in the back" by international financiers who had profited from the war and, as he thought, indirectly brought Germany to its knees. Adolf Hitler would not forget and later he would point the finger of blame at the Jews.

The great European empires of Germany, Austria-Hungary and Russia disappeared into the history books and the victorious allies set about making sure that Germany never again would threaten the international peace.

Here again the seeds of **nationalism** were sown and the lessons of history ignored. In Paris, on June 28th, 1919 the Treaty of Versailles began the process of emasculating Germany, thereby guaranteeing that, instead of being welcomed back into the brotherhood of nations, it would remain a devastated, isolated and bitter enemy. The overriding objective was that the terms offered to Germany would make it incapable of ever dominating Europe again. Clemenceau of France wanted the country brought to its knees. The British Prime Minister Lloyd George recognised that Germany could be an ally against communist Russia but public opinion at home demanded that somehow Germany should pay for what it had started. President Wilson of America just wanted reconciliation and a strong and economically viable Europe. The terms of the treaty were devastating for Germany.

- It had to admit blame for starting the war and pay $31.4 billion dollars in recompense.
- It had to limit its army to no more than 100,000 men, keep only six warships and have no submarines.
- There were no military aircraft to be allowed.
- The German west bank of the Rhine was to be occupied by allied troops.
- It was to be deprived of significant parts of its territory, including the "Polish corridor", a narrow strip of land separating Germany from East Prussia.
- In the west Alsace-Lorraine, which the Germans had won from the French in1871, was returned.
- It lost all its colonies in Africa, China and the Pacific.

Understandably there was a hostile reaction in Germany and even moderate politicians criticised the treaty as "a doctrine of hatred and delusion". During the latter stages of the war the populace had been assured by Woodrow Wilson that the enemy was not Germany but the Kaiser and the military high command. The Kaiser had abdicated at the end of the war and, after a communist uprising in 1919, a democratic republican government had been voted into office in the city of Weimar. Surely the ordinary German citizen should not be punished for the excesses of the generals?

Incensed at the terms agreed, however, and also by the fact that they weren't allowed a place at the negotiating table, the German delegation refused to show any regrets and in the closing hours the blustering, pompous Foreign Minister, Count Brockdorf-Rantzau, delivered a contemptuous speech, refusing to admit to any blame for the war whatsoever and leaving the Allied delegates shaking with fury. It was a stupid thing to do but at least it reflected the depth of feeling amongst the German people. It also gave the German right wing and its military sympathisers the confidence to denounce the Weimar republic as "November criminals" and the treaty as a "Diktat" which they would fight all the way. All across Europe as a result of fragmentation of the various empires there were now small independent states, many with large German populations deeply unhappy at being separated from what they saw as their fatherland.

Somehow the Germans had to begin repaying the vast sums demanded but they simply couldn't meet the amounts and so started to print money, referred to in the twenty first century as "quantitative easing". The result was inflation on an epic scale. A default in paying in 1923 resulted in a general strike, which only made matters worse. A loaf of bread, which had cost 250 marks in January of that year cost 200,000 marks by the following November. Paper money was now worthless. The situation got so bad that there was a story of a lost suitcase of money being found. The money was left behind but the suitcase was gone.

On the wider international scene there were hopes that the League of Nations, the forerunner of the future United Nations, set up during the Versailles Treaty, would act as a sounding board and global policeman, providing protection against aggression and arbitration over disputes. Crucially, Germany was excluded until 1926, giving resentment plenty of time to fester and, despite Wilson's efforts to join the League, the American senate vetoed his wishes. Ironically, America's isolationist policies ended only at the disaster of Pearl Harbor and the unexpected attack by the Japanese in 1941.

In Germany there was chaos as businesses went bankrupt, food was hard to come by, people's lifetime savings were eroded and thousands of workers were left stranded outside the factories. Drastic economic reforms, presided over by the Reichsbank president Dr Hjalmar Schacht began to have some impact though and unemployment began to fall.

The failure of the various democratic governments, however, had failed to prevent the rise of extremists on both sides of the political spectrum and running battles between the communists and socialists on one hand and the right wing national socialists, later the Nazis, were a common and worrying sight. There was much talk of a moral justification for dictatorship and on the 8th November 1923 Adolf Hitler and twenty five of his brown shirted Nazi followers broke up a right wing meeting in the citizens beer hall in Munich. An agitated Hitler jumped onto a table, fired a shot in the air and shouted, "The national revolution has begun!" The next day he gathered more supporters and marched through the streets to the city centre where he was challenged and stopped by the police. Someone, it was never discovered who, fired a shot and in the confusion three policemen and thirteen Nazis were killed. Hitler ran for his life but the next day he was arrested, tried and jailed for five years but was released after only five months. During his time in prison he dictated the first few chapters of his political theories "Mein Kampf" ("my struggle"). He later was able to claim that leading the attempted putsch was the proudest moment of his life.

In 1925 some sensible members of the European powers met at Locarno in Switzerland to hammer out some helpful proposals and this time Germany had an equal seat at the meetings. There was agreement that its borders with France and Belgium should return to pre-war positions and they were given allowances to negotiate the border disputes with Czechoslovakia and Poland without international interference. Some people saw this as the first step in the process of "appeasement", where the feeble minded democracies bowed to threats and bullying tactics from the rising star of German nationalism, Adolf Hitler.

Hitler had been difficult from the start. There is a photo of him in his early schooldays, arms folded, staring boldly at the camera. One teacher described him as "a gaunt, pale faced youth, arrogant and bad tempered". Already he was demanding subservience from his peers, fancying himself as something of a leader. He was born in the Austrian town of Braunau on the Bavarian border, into a reasonably well off family. His father, a customs officer, was a strict, domineering disciplinarian and there was little love lost between them, while his mother had been gentle and doting. He failed to make any impression at school and in 1908 he travelled to Vienna hoping to win entry to its famous art academy. He lived an idle life, spending hours in local cafes reading newspapers and magazines and made few attempts to find work, depending on some meagre savings and the odd cheque from home. He would sleep till midday and then mooch around the city, going for long nocturnal walks and occasionally attending the opera. He had a friend with him from his home town of Linz called August Kubizek, and they would argue long into the night with others about politics, the arts and philosophy. Even at this stage it was obvious that Hitler had an unstable, hysterical personality. He hated to be contradicted or corrected on anything and would fly into a rage when interrupted. He was incensed when he failed for the second time to be accepted by the Vienna Academy of Fine Arts, the judgement on his paintings being that they were unfit for serious consideration. He distanced himself from Kubizek and drifted from lodging to lodging, even sleeping on park benches when his money ran out. He took little interest in women, a characteristic that would last throughout his life, but he did form a strong attachment later on to a young niece when he was gaining notice as a political figure. In December 1909 he was so destitute he had to move into a homeless shelter for two months and later began a stay at a home for poor men which would last for more than two years.

There were sporadic attempts at work but his chronic laziness kept him in poverty until he discovered that he could sell small watercolour paintings of famous buildings which he copied from postcards. He made friends, if that is the correct word, with another resident of the shelter called Reinhold Hanisch who helped Hitler sell the paintings. Predictably they quarrelled, and Hitler was instrumental in getting Hanisch an eight day jail sentence after falsely accusing him of stealing his belongings. When Hitler was at the height of his powers Hanisch decided to talk to the newspapers about his one time "friend" in Vienna and to shut him up Hitler had him murdered! Now completely on his own he was trying to sell his paintings, without much success, when he was befriended by Josef Neumann, a Jew who helped him sell to Jewish shop owners. It seems that at this time Hitler had none of the manic anti-semitism that was to infect the future Nazi regime. When not trying to sell paintings he would haunt Viennese libraries and spend hours in cafes poring over newspapers and political tracts. He began to develop a fascination for Norse mythology and Wagner's operas and delved into modern philosophers, especially Nietzsche and his theories of the death of god, the perceived weaknesses of Christianity and the arrival of the superman and the strength of the will. Somehow all this random reading and musical drenching coalesced into his mind and he developed his own idiosyncratic theories, one of its pillars being his belief in the supremacy of the Aryans, the master race of blond, blue eyed Nordics who would rule the world by power and divine right. He would harangue his fellow lodgers in the men's home at length on morality, racial purity and the evils of the Jews, Jesuits, communists and freemasons who were poisoning the world. If challenged or interrupted he would go into a hysterical rage, pounding a table with his fists.

This was also the time that Hitler's violent anti-semitism and nationalistic fervour took deep root. The mayor of Vienna, Karl Lueger, was a member of the Christian Social party and criticism of the Jews was a fashionable social asset. Many of Vienna's wealthiest businessmen and professionals were Jewish and in the poorer quarters of the city there was envy and resentment at their alleged cliquishness and influence. Hitler studied Lueger closely, noting his crafty use of innuendo, speech making, and ability to sway opinion through subtle propaganda. A seminal moment came in a chance encounter in an inner city street when he came face to face with an old, black robed, bearded Jew.

"I observed the man furtively and cautiously. But the moment I stared at his foreign face, scrutinising feature for feature, the more my first question assumed a new form: is this a German?"

From that moment on Hitler's anti-semitism gathered pace and he complemented it with a fierce nationalism which excluded all but the purest in blood from inclusion.

Still aimlessly drifting, he moved to Munich in 1913 and joined the 16th Bavarian Reserve Infantry at the start of the First World War.

There is a famous photo of a cheering Munich crowd, overjoyed at the announcement of hostilities, and Hitler's face can just be seen in the middle of it, grinning with delight at the news. He later wrote that the thought of war exhilarated him.

"It was like a redemption from the vexatious experience of my youth. In a transport of enthusiasm, I sank down on my knees and thanked Heaven from an overflowing heart."

He spent four years, mainly near the front line, as a "runner", a dangerous role where he had to convey messages to various positions, often under shell and sniper fire. Aloof, dogmatic in opinion and humourless – his companions thought him odd, yet his bravery won their respect and he was eventually made a lance corporal in late 1914. In 1916 he was wounded in the leg and awarded the Iron Cross, First Class, a significant honour for a mere lance corporal.

The German surrender in 1918, however, intensified his hatred of democratic politicians and international financiers whom he blamed for the "stab in the back" and he quickly joined the tiny German Workers' Party which later developed into the Nazi party. His speech making, filled with hate, vicious anti-semitic rhetoric and peppered with short, repetitive phrases, soon gained him attention and within two years he became the official party leader. After the failed putsch described earlier he tightened his grip on the party, ruthlessly eliminating any opposition and formed his own private army, the Schutzstaffel, or SS. In the 1932 general election the nationalist policies of the Nazis helped them win 232 seats, making them the largest party in Germany, and President Hindenburg invited Hitler to serve as Vice Chancellor. To be fair to the electorate, few of them had any idea of the depth of his anti-semitism, his desire for revenge on the democracies and the expansion of the Germanic race eastwards, though if they had read "Mein Kampf" more closely the clues were there. Hitler later manoeuvred himself into the Chancellorship itself in 1933 and his fist step was to destroy the Reichstag and call for more elections to increase his powers. To achieve this he bullied his way to the ballot box by suppressing opposition newspapers, disrupting other political meetings, even having their speakers beaten up by his own Stormtroopers. One of his deputies, Hermann Goring, expressed the Nazi contempt for free speech and democratic principles unequivocally: "I don't have to worry about justice. My mission is only to destroy and exterminate, nothing more."

Those blunt, chilling sentences captured the essence of Nazi thinking, if it can be called that. Brutality, force, the goose step, the crushing of any opposition, genocide and a complete suspension of democratic principles were the key factors that led to another world war. Extreme nationalism, a blind loathing of other races and cultures and a refusal to honour treaties and diplomatic initiatives were to blame. Added to that list would be the inept reaction of the other European democracies which failed to stand up to Hitler all the way through the 1930s He had vowed to undo the humiliations of the Versailles Treaty and in 1935 launched a huge rearmament programme that the European leaders, apart from the prophetic but at the time powerless Winston Churchill, simply ignored. He then reoccupied the Rhineland and formed an alliance with the Italian nationalist dictator Mussolini. In the same year he signed the Anti-Comintern pact with Japan to halt the spread of communism. When Italy signed it as well the formation of the future axis powers was complete. Hitler then annexed Austria, installing a puppet government, and then Czechoslovakia which became a German "protectorate". Hitler had totally bewildered the French, British and Czech Prime Ministers, making outrageous demands, giving ground, then offering outright lies. The chief "appeaser" was Neville Chamberlain, the British P.M. who flew twice to Germany and came back convinced he had a peace treaty. He had reassuring words for Parliament: "There has come back from Germany peace with honour. I believe it is peace for our time." He was hopelessly deluded, however, in assuming that Hitler would keep his word and honour the treaty. In Parliament Winston Churchill was unconvinced and prophesied that dark times were ahead, possibly for the entire world: "England has been offered a choice, between war and shame," he growled. "She has chosen shame and will get war."

Chapter Fourteen

JASTA. SUMMARY AND CONCLUSION

It is ninety nine years since the end of the First World War and seventy two since the end of the second one. The first ushered in challenges to the liberal political consensus, and the second saw the defeat of fascism. Since then we have had no universal catastrophe to equal them, though the world stared into a nuclear abyss in 1962 when John Kennedy and Nikita Khrushchev brought us to the edge of a third world war.

My argument throughout the book has been that there are chilling parallels between those times, and the current political mood. The reappearance of nationalism and the fragmentation of the global empires of the time find echoes in today's surge towards independence and rejection of international institutions and political elites. The JASTA Act, with its direct challenge to sovereignty, could result in a similar rebirth of defensive nationalism and has therefore the potential to recreate the conditions that ushered in those two world wars.

The international condemnation of the act is gathering pace, as realisation of its damaging consequences becomes clear. The fact that JASTA will give an opportunity for individual citizens around the world to sue many other sovereign nations, including the US, is prompting furious reaction.

The Saudi Foreign Ministry announced that JASTA would "contribute to the erosion of the principle of sovereign immunity, the bedrock or cornerstone of conduct in international relations". A French Foreign Ministry spokesman, Romain Nadal, claimed that it would violate international law, and he was echoed by Ahmed Abu Zaid, a spokesman for Egypt's Foreign Ministry, who argued that it could have a dire effect on international relations. Bahrain's Foreign Minister, Sheikh Khaled bin Ahmed, tweeted rhetorically "Are there no rational people among you?" and added that JASTA "is an arrow launched by the US congress at its own country". The Dutch Parliament said that JASTA is a "gross and unwarranted breach of Dutch sovereignty".

Severe criticism also came from President Obama when he was still in office. He called it a "mistake" and "basically a political vote". His Press Secretary, John Earnest, agreed:

"The concern that we have is simply this: It could put the United Sates, our taxpayers and our service members and our diplomats at significant risk if countries were to adopt a similar law. Let me give you one example. Obviously, the United States is involved in a wide variety of humanitarian relief efforts in countries around the world at any given time. If someone decided that they were unhappy with the way that those humanitarian relief efforts were being carried out, you could imagine that someone in a faraway country could file a lawsuit against the US".

In my opinion this almost universal criticism is totally justified, as JASTA is flying in the face of international protocol and common sense. It is in direct conflict with the fundamental principles of international law and sovereign immunity and if the US congress is wise enough it should be immediately repealed.

It can also be argued that JASTA could be a threat to the very existence of democracy itself. This may sound like extremist nonsense but democracy as a legitimate form of government is going through a troublesome time at the moment with populist movements around the globe expressing their frustrations with establishment figures by voting them out of office.

So will the passing of the JASTA Act threaten the survival of democracy? If the sovereignty of a country is under intense pressure to protect itself from independent legal claims won't there be a feeling that it must come together to defend itself, and that it will need strong authoritative leaders to answer or rebuff the charges?

The skies seem to be darkening for these liberal democracies as authoritarianism gains a hold on the political scene. There are numerous countries around the world which still pretend that the ballot box is the ultimate decider, but freedom of speech, a free press and human rights are missing in these so called "democracies".

In many countries autocracy is back, with mass arrests of judges and journalists and corruption is giving democracy a bad name. 25% of young Americans are giving a thumbs down to it and half of that percentage would welcome a military takeover in the event of more government incompetence. The Arab spring eventually gave way to the Arab winter with little change in countries' economic performance or national outlook. In the UK there was a huge turnout in the referendum on leaving the EU but it now has little effective political opposition. The British historian Andrew Roberts summed it all up during a speech to an American audience, arguing that democracy was in retreat and was losing across "huge swathes of Asia and Africa" as populist, right of centre groups gather momentum.

I also feel that a headlong retreat into nationalism or populism can morph into a form of isolationism, but "My country right or wrong" has never, in my opinion, been a healthy outlook as it encourages an international free-for-all, a dog eat dog mentality with no moral centre, and this is another reason why I feel the JASTA act could be so dangerous unless it is repealed. By its very nature JASTA will instil a reactionary approach in states that feel threatened by its aggressive approach to their sovereignty and anarchy could be loosed upon the world.

Contrary to popular opinion I think the US has never been happy in its role as a universal policeman, but if it loses confidence in its values and withdraws into isolationism then the vacuum could be filled by something else, such as maverick states or extremist groups that feel they can challenge the stability of the world by pursuing their own aggressive agendas, regardless of the outcome.

There is, for example, a plan published recently by the South Korean Defence Ministry which promises "Massive Punishment and Retaliation" as soon as a North Korean nuclear attack is identified. It warns that the North Korean capital Pyongyang, a city of 2.5 million, will be "reduced to ashes and removed from the map". This is horrific enough but fast forward to China's reaction. Would North Korea's ally sit back as if nothing had happened? Would the US remain impotent and silent, or would it enter the field to attempt to prevent a third world war?

I believe therefore that we abandon democracy at our peril because it has been the very thing that has managed to keep the peace between the major power blocks and it is still humanity's best choice for maintaining a lasting peace. Winston Churchill's quote that it is the best form of government still holds true today, despite the risk of nationalist fervour morphing into aggression towards other countries. The economic argument for democracy is formidable, as the freedoms it enshrines allow for confidence, stability and transparency. It is true that for a while a dictatorship can produce initial growth but in the long run corruption is a certainty and wealth tends to end up in the hands of the elite. Hitler revived the Germany economy and built the autobahns, and Mussolini made the trains run on schedule, but they were both on borrowed time as the gross absurdities and brutalities of their regimes became clear and the human spirit began to reassert itself in reaction to slavery and tyranny.

Democracy, in direct contrast to dictatorship, encourages long term investment and trade, provides schools and hospitals, permits religious freedom, and harmonises social unrest. It has served mankind well in the past and it would be a retrograde step to allow an act like JASTA to undermine or even destroy it.

As I emphasised in the previous chapter, nationalism in its true form can be a positive force for good but if it drifts into a narrow extremism it can be brutal and aggressive. Hence the importance of challenging JASTA before it forces countries into these defensive stances.

So why are the liberal values of freedom and tolerance, which triumphed over Nazism and communism in the twentieth century, and, until recently, were admired as the most enlightened form of government, being rejected in favour of nationalism? Why are they unable to attract the best of the best as leaders and why in some cases is there a preference for autocracy?

"We have nothing to fear but fear itself" was President Roosevelt's rallying cry to Americans trapped in the deadly depression of the thirties. Maybe there is the same "fear" today as confidence in the values of democracy ebb away.

In previous chapters I have alluded to some responses to this question, but the political landscape is changing so quickly that it is difficult to give concrete answers.

In 1992 Francis Fukuyama proposed an "end of history" thesis to popular acclaim. The bloodless break-up of the Soviet Union, he claimed, was a thrilling testament to the universalisation of western liberal democratic values and we were living at "the end point of mankind's ideological evolution". Democracy would be the final form of government for everyone as all over the world people were yearning for freedom, for free markets, for freedom of expression, for equal rights and an end to racial or sexual discrimination. The values of the West would permeate and enrich the entire globe and universal peace would at last be achieved. For a brief period there was global optimism that we were living in a democratic heaven, liberated from the cold war and ideological struggles. Then came the invasion of Iraq, the war in Afghanistan, 9/11. These were wake-up calls to the fact that history doesn't run to a pre-planned narrative and will take its own unpredictable course. The Bush-Blair partnership still believed that the rest of the world was ready to greet democracy with open arms, but the aftermath of the Iraq invasion, and later the failure of the Arab spring to reach any far reaching reforms, demolished their hopes.

Earlier, there had been two huge blows that rocked confidence in the democratic process; the first was the financial crisis of 2007-08 and then the dramatic growth of China as an economic superpower. It was only the timely intervention of some swift thinking politicians that averted a world-wide recession, but the after effects of the crisis were still devastating. Capitalism seemed to be in retreat and the old Marxist prediction of its ultimate failure as a system seemed to be relevant, despite its own contradictions and collapse. Democratic governments had been trying to live up to their election promises by borrowing huge sums of money, with the complacent assumption that the resulting growth would help to pay off the debts. They then bailed out the failing banks with taxpayers' money and stood by while the financiers paid themselves massive bonuses before retiring from the scene.

At the same time, China, well distanced from the crisis, was doubling its living standards by the decade. It was busy stage managing capitalism's great ideas with a corresponding tightly controlled communist ethos. Its spectacular success didn't go unnoticed in the outer world and was in itself a challenge to the supremacy of democracy. There was a price to pay of course. Any form of dissent was forbidden, including a free press, and all the rules of the game were dictated from on high. In the long run this could have unforeseen consequences. In 2016, acting against the advice of many of his economists to proceed with moderate growth, President Xi Jinping ordered a minimum 6.5 per cent gross domestic product target for the following five years. This was widely seen as economic insanity but without an opposition voice, as in democracy, the decree was unchallengeable. The only way that this target could be achieved was by massive borrowing, ploughing money into the economy in a frantic effort to keep growth going. To be fair at present the system seems to be working but many experts believe that within about five years there will be a debt implosion and a possible Chinese recession. If this ever happened the consequences for the rest of the world, which relies on Chinese demand for its goods and cheap ones in return, are not difficult to work out; it would be a lose-lose situation. In addition to a looming financial crisis, according to a report in The Economist magazine, China is developing a super rich elite with the fifty wealthiest members of The National People's Congress worth $94.7 billion, sixty times as much as the fifty richest members of America's Congress.

Another setback for democracy was in Russia when the fall of communism raised hopes for a revival of freedom. Boris Yeltsin started the process but was easily outmanoeuvred by Vladimir Putin, a former KGB officer whose championing of Russia's history and Christian heritage has made him a popular figure, despite his autocratic style of government.

Then there is Iraq. George Bush and the neo-cons in America just assumed that if they overthrew Saddam Hussein then the country would express its thanks by welcoming democracy as its saviour. It was not to be. The raison d'etre of the 2003 invasion, the weapons of mass destruction, were nowhere to be found but the argument held that the establishing of democracy was the ultimate justification. The resulting chaos was seized upon by his critics as proof that this was all just a disguise to safeguard the oil supplies and that democracy couldn't just "grow"; it had to have historical roots as a necessary foundation.

Much the same thing happened in Egypt with the collapse in 2011 of the Hosni Mubarak regime. This coincided with the upsurge of the Arab Spring and there were tremendous hopes that the country could hold genuine, corruption free elections and establish a real democracy. It managed to do so but within only a few months, the legally elected government of Mohammed Morsi's Muslim Brotherhood was already causing concern, allegedly abusing its mandate by stacking the state with "Brothers". Morsi's time in power was short enough to confirm these and in 2013 the army put a stop to things by arresting him, a situation which led to the deaths of hundreds of demonstrators. The brief flowering of democracy, allowed to bloom in many Middle East states, finally withered.

It was the same story in much of the wider world, with respect for the gifts of free elections, government accountability and transparency in freefall. In Turkey the once westward looking party of President Erdogan is turning towards the East seeking an alliance with Russia, has dropped its requests for admission to the

EU and is rediscovering its Islamic roots. In South Africa there were rumblings of discontent about the African National Congress's monopoly on power and the amount of taxpayers' money allegedly being spent on the households of some leading ministers.

In South America many countries are waving goodbye to socialism, with a shift towards the centre right. Ecuador's election will probably see the end of the left wing populist Rafael Correa and in Chile the same will most likely apply to the socialist government of Michelle Bachelet. There is a growing economic crisis in Venezuela where the inflation rate has risen to ludicrously high figures, leading to the National Assembly voting for a political trial against President Nicolas Maduro. He has been trying to continue with the socialist policies of former president Chavez but the opposition parties are claiming that the revenue from Venezuela's huge oil reserves are allegedly being mismanaged and democratic freedoms are being eroded.

There are similar feelings within the EU countries where unelected technocrats make crucial decisions without consulting the populace at large. The introduction of the Euro for example was just "announced" in 1999, even though two countries which held referendums on the matter, Denmark and Sweden, both voted "no". The running joke is that these referendums should be held again and again until the ignorant people arrive at the "correct" decision. There were brief flirtations with democracy when the EU elite courted popular opinion on the Lisbon Treaty, which was designed to give more power to Brussels, but the process was quietly dropped when the people again voted the "wrong" way. It is no wonder that feelings of alienation and frustrations are manifested when genuine concerns about immigration, terrorism, low economic growth and demographic decline are ignored by a remote, and unaccountable elite.

So democracy is facing attacks from both without and within. The challenges from within arrive when a country has enjoyed long years of freedom of speech, transparent elections and government accountability and a tendency for complacency settles in. If this is accompanied by amnesia about the past, general ignorance of the long and painful routes that had to be overcome to achieve that level of political independence and prosperity, then powerful challenges will begin to take shape.

The amnesia is sadly running riot in the higher reaches of academia. In 1987 Allan Bloom, a distinguished American academic, published a bestselling book called "The closing of the American Mind". In it he argued that Western universities had abandoned their principles and their purpose and were impoverishing the souls of their pupils. The heart of his thesis was that the original aim of the university was to have been an island of intellectual freedom, where all views were investigated without restriction or exclusion. Liberal democracy made this possible, but, in his opinion, the universities have become inundated with the backflow of society's problems and now spend much of their time censoring what they see as unacceptable social or political views, with civilised discourse a thing of the past. For the past forty years or so this transmission of a supposedly liberal education has been accompanied by an astonishing ignorance of historical knowledge. He claims that the modern student is as intelligent as any of his or her predecessors, but is lacking in intellectual curiosity and is woefully ignorant of the past, in particular his or her country's struggle to attain the freedoms of democracy.

Test scores from the National Assessment of Educational Progress in 2010, for example, revealed that only 35% of fourth graders knew the purpose of the Declaration of Independence, and other studies showed that only about 25% of teenagers were able to correctly identity Adolf Hitler as Germany's leader in World War

Two. It isn't just history. I know of a university graduate in the UK who was setting out on a rugby trip to Dubai. His girlfriend, also a university graduate, asked if she could come with him as she'd "never been to America".

If we accept George Orwell's principle that "he who controls the past controls the present and he who controls the present controls the future" then educational dysfunction on this scale doesn't make for much confidence in the primacy of a sound liberal democracy.

Minority groups can suddenly appear, emboldened by like-minded chatter on the internet. Scotland demands independence from the UK, the Catalans from Spain, regional mayors push for more influence, and fragmentation of the state is threatened. This is the attack from within.

It still remains to be seen what effect President Trump's flurry of executive orders in his first week of office will have on the democratic process. His policy on Obama's health care programme, his temporary banning of Muslim immigrants and his commitment to build a wall across the Mexican border, among others, have resulted in unprecedented levels of criticism both at home and abroad. I hope that as he continues in office he keeps his promises to the electorate who voted him in but that he listens to his advisors before distancing himself too far from those who didn't vote for him. As he said in his first press conference when referring to a divided country: "We have to come together."

Taking all these factors into account, it is clear that democracy, with its attendant freedoms of expression and belief, is facing a crisis. JASTA will pose an immediate threat but political correctness is already beginning to erode some of these hard won basic rights. The arrival of populist politicians, fundamentalism and right wing extremism needs to be faced down and challenged by the genuine strengths of its enduring principles. In the memorable words of Winston Churchill: "Democracy is the worst from of government, except for all those other forms that have been tried from time to time."

Tarek El-Tayeb Mohamed Bouazizi
(1984-2011)

A young Tunisian street vendor who set himself on fire on 17th December 2011 in protest at the humiliating confiscation of his goods by a local official and her aides. His suicide was instrumental in inciting demonstrations against autocratic governments throughout the Middle East during the "Arab Spring" of 2012

Arab Spring

Mass demonstrations in Tahir Square, Cairo, in support of the 'Arab Spring' in 2012

Arab Spring

Mass demonstrations in Tahir Square, Cairo, in support of the 'Arab Spring' in 2012

Kashmir conflict

Since the partition of British India in 1947 and the creation of India and Pakistan the two countries have been involved in a series of wars and conflicts. Both countries possess nuclear weapons and have threatened to use them in extreme circumstances

North Korea

North Korea Supreme Leader Kim Jong-un revealed in 2013 that plans for conducting nuclear strikes on US cities, including Los Angeles and Washington DC, were underway but intelligence reports suggest that the country currently lacks missiles strong enough to deliver them

The Israeli / Palestinian conflict

*The Israeli / Palestinian conflict has been raging for over half a century.
Here a member of the Israel Defense Force stands guard in Nablus*

The Israeli / Palestinian conflict

A young Palestinian boy stands in front of destroyed houses in the Gaza strip, March 2009

Vladimir Putin

Prime Minister of Russia (2008-2012) and President of The Russian Federation since 2012. He claims to have brought stability to the country and restored its sense of national pride but some are critical of his autocratic style of leadership

Donald Trump

Unprecedented election to office of a man with no political experience, who has promised to "make America great again", but he faces stiff opposition from the defeated Democratic party and even from some of his own Republicans

Appendix 1

THE JASTA LAW

'Justice Against Sponsors of Terrorism Act'

(Sec. 3) This bill amends the federal judicial code to narrow the scope of foreign sovereign immunity (i.e., a foreign state's immunity from the jurisdiction of U.S. courts).

Specifically, it authorizes federal court jurisdiction over a civil claim against a foreign state for physical injury to a person or property or death that occurs inside the United States as a result of: (1) an act of international terrorism, and (2) a tort committed anywhere by an official, agent, or employee of a foreign state acting within the scope of employment.

International terrorism does not include an act of war. Federal court jurisdiction does not extend to a tort claim based on an omission or an act that is merely negligent.

A U.S. national may file a civil action against a foreign state for physical injury, death, or damage as a result of an act of international terrorism committed by a designated terrorist organization.

(Sec. 4) The bill amends the federal criminal code to impose civil liability on a person who conspires to commit or aids and abets (by knowingly providing substantial assistance) an act of international terrorism committed, planned, or authorized by a designated terrorist organization.

(Sec. 5) It establishes exclusive federal court jurisdiction over civil claims under this bill.

It authorizes the Department of Justice (DOJ) to intervene in civil proceedings to seek a stay. A court may grant the stay if the Department of State certifies that the United States is engaged in good-faith discussions with the foreign state to resolve the civil claims.

(Sec. 7) This bill's amendments apply to a civil claim: (1) pending on or commenced on or after enactment; and (2) arising out of an injury to a person, property, or business on or after September 11, 2001.

Appendix 2

UN CHARTER

WE THE PEOPLES OF THE UNITED NATIONS
DETERMINED

- to save succeeding generations from the scourge of war, which twice in our lifetime has brought untold sorrow to mankind, and
- to reaffirm faith in fundamental human rights, in the dignity and worth of the human person, in the equal rights of men and women and of nations large and small, and
- to establish conditions under which justice and respect for the obligations arising from treaties and other sources of international law can be maintained, and
- to promote social progress and better standards of life in larger freedom,

AND FOR THESE ENDS

- to practice tolerance and live together in peace with one another as good neighbours, and
- to unite our strength to maintain international peace and security, and
- to ensure, by the acceptance of principles and the institution of methods, that armed force shall not be used, save in the common interest, and

- to employ international machinery for the promotion of the economic and social advancement of all peoples,

HAVE RESOLVED TO COMBINE OUR EFFORTS TO ACCOMPLISH THESE AIMS

Accordingly, our respective Governments, through representatives assembled in the city of San Francisco, who have exhibited their full powers found to be in good and due form, have agreed to the present Charter of the United Nations and do hereby establish an international organization to be known as the United Nations.

CHAPTER I: PURPOSES AND PRINCIPLES

Article 1
The Purposes of the United Nations are:

1. To maintain international peace and security, and to that end: to take effective collective measures for the prevention and removal of threats to the peace, and for the suppression of acts of aggression or other breaches of the peace, and to bring about by peaceful means, and in conformity with the principles of justice and international law, adjustment or settlement of international disputes or situations which might lead to a breach of the peace;
2. To develop friendly relations among nations based on respect for the principle of equal rights and self-determination of peoples, and to take other appropriate measures to strengthen universal peace;
3. To achieve international co-operation in solving international problems of an economic, social, cultural, or humanitarian character, and in promoting and encouraging respect for human rights and for fundamental freedoms for all without distinction as to race, sex, language, or religion; and

4. To be a centre for harmonizing the actions of nations in the attainment of these common ends.

Article 2

1. The Organization and its Members, in pursuit of the Purposes stated in Article 1, shall act in accordance with the following Principles.
2. The Organization is based on the principle of the sovereign equality of all its Members.
3. All Members, in order to ensure to all of them the rights and benefits resulting from membership, shall fulfill in good faith the obligations assumed by them in accordance with the present Charter.
4. All Members shall settle their international disputes by peaceful means in such a manner that international peace and security, and justice, are not endangered.
5. All Members shall refrain in their international relations from the threat or use of force against the territorial integrity or political independence of any state, or in any other manner inconsistent with the Purposes of the United Nations.
6. All Members shall give the United Nations every assistance in any action it takes in accordance with the present Charter, and shall refrain from giving assistance to any state against which the United Nations is taking preventive or enforcement action.
7. The Organization shall ensure that states which are not Members of the United Nations act in accordance with these Principles so far as may be necessary for the maintenance of international peace and security.
8. Nothing contained in the present Charter shall authorize the United Nations to intervene in matters which are essentially within the domestic jurisdiction of any state or shall require the Members to submit such matters to settlement under the present Charter; but this principle shall not prejudice the application of enforcement measures under Chapter Vll.

CHAPTER II: MEMBERSHIP

Article 3
The original Members of the United Nations shall be the states which, having participated in the United Nations Conference on International Organization at San Francisco, or having previously signed the Declaration by United Nations of 1 January 1942, sign the present Charter and ratify it in accordance with Article 110.

Article 4
1. Membership in the United Nations is open to all other peace-loving states which accept the obligations contained in the present Charter and, in the judgment of the Organization, are able and willing to carry out these obligations.
2. The admission of any such state to membership in the United Nations will be effected by a decision of the General Assembly upon the recommendation of the Security Council.

Article 5
A Member of the United Nations against which preventive or enforcement action has been taken by the Security Council may be suspended from the exercise of the rights and privileges of membership by the General Assembly upon the recommendation of the Security Council. The exercise of these rights and privileges may be restored by the Security Council.

Article 6
A Member of the United Nations which has persistently violated the Principles contained in the present Charter may be expelled from the Organization by the General Assembly upon the recommendation of the Security Council.

CHAPTER III: ORGANS

Article 7
1. There are established as principal organs of the United Nations: a General Assembly, a Security Council, an Economic and Social Council, a Trusteeship Council, an International Court of Justice and a Secretariat.
2. Such subsidiary organs as may be found necessary may be established in accordance with the present Charter.

Article 8
The United Nations shall place no restrictions on the eligibility of men and women to participate in any capacity and under conditions of equality in its principal and subsidiary organs.

CHAPTER IV: THE GENERAL ASSEMBLY

COMPOSITION

Article 9
1. The General Assembly shall consist of all the Members of the United Nations.
2. Each Member shall have not more than five representatives in the General Assembly.

FUNCTIONS and POWERS

Article 10
The General Assembly may discuss any questions or any matters within the scope of the present Charter or relating to the powers and functions of any organs provided for in the present Charter, and, except as provided in Article 12, may make recommendations to the Members of the United Nations or to the Security Council or to both on any such questions or matters.

Article 11

1. The General Assembly may consider the general principles of co-operation in the maintenance of international peace and security, including the principles governing disarmament and the regulation of armaments, and may make recommendations with regard to such principles to the Members or to the Security Council or to both.

2. The General Assembly may discuss any questions relating to the maintenance of international peace and security brought before it by any Member of the United Nations, or by the Security Council, or by a state which is not a Member of the United Nations in accordance with Article 35, paragraph 2, and, except as provided in Article 12, may make recommendations with regard to any such questions to the state or states concerned or to the Security Council or to both. Any such question on which action is necessary shall be referred to the Security Council by the General Assembly either before or after discussion.

3. The General Assembly may call the attention of the Security Council to situations which are likely to endanger international peace and security.

4. The powers of the General Assembly set forth in this Article shall not limit the general scope of Article 10.

Article 12

1. While the Security Council is exercising in respect of any dispute or situation the functions assigned to it in the present Charter, the General Assembly shall not make any recommendation with regard to that dispute or situation unless the Security Council so requests.

2. The Secretary-General, with the consent of the Security Council, shall notify the General Assembly at each session of any matters relative to the maintenance of international peace and security which are being dealt with by the Security Council and shall similarly notify the General Assembly, or

the Members of the United Nations if the General Assembly is not in session, immediately the Security Council ceases to deal with such matters.

Article 13

1. The General Assembly shall initiate studies and make recommendations for the purpose of:
   a. promoting international co-operation in the political field and encouraging the progressive development of international law and its codification;
   b. promoting international co-operation in the economic, social, cultural, educational, and health fields, and assisting in the realization of human rights and fundamental freedoms for all without distinction as to race, sex, language, or religion.
   c. The further responsibilities, functions and powers of the General Assembly with respect to matters mentioned in paragraph 1 (b) above are set forth in Chapters IX and X.

Article 14

Subject to the provisions of Article 12, the General Assembly may recommend measures for the peaceful adjustment of any situation, regardless of origin, which it deems likely to impair the general welfare or friendly relations among nations, including situations resulting from a violation of the provisions of the present Charter setting forth the Purposes and Principles of the United Nations.

Article 15

1. The General Assembly shall receive and consider annual and special reports from the Security Council; these reports shall include an account of the measures that the Security Council has decided upon or taken to maintain international peace and security.
2. The General Assembly shall receive and consider reports from

the other organs of the United Nations.

Article 16
The General Assembly shall perform such functions with respect to the international trusteeship system as are assigned to it under Chapters XII and XIII, including the approval of the trusteeship agreements for areas not designated as strategic.

Article 17
1. The General Assembly shall consider and approve the budget of the Organization.
2. The expenses of the Organization shall be borne by the Members as apportioned by the General Assembly.
3. The General Assembly shall consider and approve any financial and budgetary arrangements with specialized agencies referred to in Article 57 and shall examine the administrative budgets of such specialized agencies with a view to making recommendations to the agencies concerned.

VOTING

Article 18
1. Each member of the General Assembly shall have one vote.
2. Decisions of the General Assembly on important questions shall be made by a two-thirds majority of the members present and voting. These questions shall include: recommendations with respect to the maintenance of international peace and security, the election of the non-permanent members of the Security Council, the election of the members of the Economic and Social Council, the election of members of the Trusteeship Council in accordance with paragraph 1 (c) of Article 86, the admission of new Members to the United Nations, the suspension of the rights and privileges of membership, the expulsion of Members, questions relating to the operation of

the trusteeship system, and budgetary questions.

3. Decisions on other questions, including the determination of additional categories of questions to be decided by a two-thirds majority, shall be made by a majority of the members present and voting.

Article 19
A Member of the United Nations which is in arrears in the payment of its financial contributions to the Organization shall have no vote in the General Assembly if the amount of its arrears equals or exceeds the amount of the contributions due from it for the preceding two full years. The General Assembly may, nevertheless, permit such a Member to vote if it is satisfied that the failure to pay is due to conditions beyond the control of the Member.

PROCEDURE

Article 20
The General Assembly shall meet in regular annual sessions and in such special sessions as occasion may require. Special sessions shall be convoked by the Secretary-General at the request of the Security Council or of a majority of the Members of the United Nations.

Article 21
The General Assembly shall adopt its own rules of procedure. It shall elect its President for each session.

Article 22
The General Assembly may establish such subsidiary organs as it deems necessary for the performance of its functions.

CHAPTER V: THE SECURITY COUNCIL

COMPOSITION

Article 23

1. The Security Council shall consist of fifteen Members of the United Nations. The Republic of China, France, the Union of Soviet Socialist Republics, the United Kingdom of Great Britain and Northern Ireland, and the United States of America shall be permanent members of the Security Council. The General Assembly shall elect ten other Members of the United Nations to be non-permanent members of the Security Council, due regard being specially paid, in the first instance to the contribution of Members of the United Nations to the maintenance of international peace and security and to the other purposes of the Organization, and also to equitable geographical distribution.

2. The non-permanent members of the Security Council shall be elected for a term of two years. In the first election of the non-permanent members after the increase of the membership of the Security Council from eleven to fifteen, two of the four additional members shall be chosen for a term of one year. A retiring member shall not be eligible for immediate re-election.

3. Each member of the Security Council shall have one representative.

FUNCTIONS and POWERS

Article 24

1. In order to ensure prompt and effective action by the United Nations, its Members confer on the Security Council primary responsibility for the maintenance of international peace and security, and agree that in carrying out its duties under this responsibility the Security Council acts on their behalf.

2. In discharging these duties the Security Council shall act in accordance with the Purposes and Principles of the United Nations. The specific powers granted to the Security Council for the discharge of these duties are laid down in Chapters VI, VII, VIII, and XII.
3. The Security Council shall submit annual and, when necessary, special reports to the General Assembly for its consideration.

Article 25
The Members of the United Nations agree to accept and carry out the decisions of the Security Council in accordance with the present Charter.

Article 26
In order to promote the establishment and maintenance of international peace and security with the least diversion for armaments of the world's human and economic resources, the Security Council shall be responsible for formulating, with the assistance of the Military Staff Committee referred to in Article 47, plans to be submitted to the Members of the United Nations for the establishment of a system for the regulation of armaments.

VOTING

Article 27
1. Each member of the Security Council shall have one vote.
2. Decisions of the Security Council on procedural matters shall be made by an affirmative vote of nine members.
3. Decisions of the Security Council on all other matters shall be made by an affirmative vote of nine members including the concurring votes of the permanent members; provided that, in decisions under Chapter VI, and under paragraph 3 of Article 52, a party to a dispute shall abstain from voting.

PROCEDURE

Article 28

1. The Security Council shall be so organized as to be able to function continuously. Each member of the Security Council shall for this purpose be represented at all times at the seat of the Organization.
2. The Security Council shall hold periodic meetings at which each of its members may, if it so desires, be represented by a member of the government or by some other specially designated representative.
3. The Security Council may hold meetings at such places other than the seat of the Organization as in its judgment will best facilitate its work.

Article 29

The Security Council may establish such subsidiary organs as it deems necessary for the performance of its functions.

Article 30

The Security Council shall adopt its own rules of procedure, including the method of selecting its President.

Article 31

Any Member of the United Nations which is not a member of the Security Council may participate, without vote, in the discussion of any question brought before the Security Council whenever the latter considers that the interests of that Member are specially affected.

Article 32

Any Member of the United Nations which is not a member of the Security Council or any state which is not a Member of the United Nations, if it is a party to a dispute under consideration by the

Security Council, shall be invited to participate, without vote, in the discussion relating to the dispute. The Security Council shall lay down such conditions as it deems just for the participation of a state which is not a Member of the United Nations.

CHAPTER VI: PACIFIC SETTLEMENT OF DISPUTES

Article 33
1. The parties to any dispute, the continuance of which is likely to endanger the maintenance of international peace and security, shall, first of all, seek a solution by negotiation, enquiry, mediation, conciliation, arbitration, judicial settlement, resort to regional agencies or arrangements, or other peaceful means of their own choice.
2. The Security Council shall, when it deems necessary, call upon the parties to settle their dispute by such means.

Article 34
The Security Council may investigate any dispute, or any situation which might lead to international friction or give rise to a dispute, in order to determine whether the continuance of the dispute or situation is likely to endanger the maintenance of international peace and security.

Article 35
1. Any Member of the United Nations may bring any dispute, or any situation of the nature referred to in Article 34, to the attention of the Security Council or of the General Assembly.
2. A state which is not a Member of the United Nations may bring to the attention of the Security Council or of the General Assembly any dispute to which it is a party if it accepts in advance, for the purposes of the dispute, the obligations of pacific settlement provided in the present Charter.

3. The proceedings of the General Assembly in respect of matters brought to its attention under this Article will be subject to the provisions of Articles 11 and 12.

Article 36

1. The Security Council may, at any stage of a dispute of the nature referred to in Article 33 or of a situation of like nature, recommend appropriate procedures or methods of adjustment.
2. The Security Council should take into consideration any procedures for the settlement of the dispute which have already been adopted by the parties.
3. In making recommendations under this Article the Security Council should also take into consideration that legal disputes should as a general rule be referred by the parties to the International Court of Justice in accordance with the provisions of the Statute of the Court.

Article 37

1. Should the parties to a dispute of the nature referred to in Article 33 fail to settle it by the means indicated in that Article, they shall refer it to the Security Council.
2. If the Security Council deems that the continuance of the dispute is in fact likely to endanger the maintenance of international peace and security, it shall decide whether to take action under Article 36 or to recommend such terms of settlement as it may consider appropriate.

Article 38

Without prejudice to the provisions of Articles 33 to 37, the Security Council may, if all the parties to any dispute so request, make recommendations to the parties with a view to a pacific settlement of the dispute.

CHAPTER VII: ACTION WITH RESPECT TO THREATS TO THE PEACE, BREACHES OF THE PEACE, AND ACTS OF AGGRESSION

Article 39
The Security Council shall determine the existence of any threat to the peace, breach of the peace, or act of aggression and shall make recommendations, or decide what measures shall be taken in accordance with Articles 41 and 42, to maintain or restore international peace and security.

Article 40
In order to prevent an aggravation of the situation, the Security Council may, before making the recommendations or deciding upon the measures provided for in Article 39, call upon the parties concerned to comply with such provisional measures as it deems necessary or desirable. Such provisional measures shall be without prejudice to the rights, claims, or position of the parties concerned. The Security Council shall duly take account of failure to comply with such provisional measures.

Article 41
The Security Council may decide what measures not involving the use of armed force are to be employed to give effect to its decisions, and it may call upon the Members of the United Nations to apply such measures. These may include complete or partial interruption of economic relations and of rail, sea, air, postal, telegraphic, radio, and other means of communication, and the severance of diplomatic relations.

Article 42
Should the Security Council consider that measures provided for in Article 41 would be inadequate or have proved to be inadequate, it may take such action by air, sea, or land forces as may be necessary

to maintain or restore international peace and security. Such action may include demonstrations, blockade, and other operations by air, sea, or land forces of Members of the United Nations.

Article 43

1. All Members of the United Nations, in order to contribute to the maintenance of international peace and security, undertake to make available to the Security Council, on its call and in accordance with a special agreement or agreements, armed forces, assistance, and facilities, including rights of passage, necessary for the purpose of maintaining international peace and security.
2. Such agreement or agreements shall govern the numbers and types of forces, their degree of readiness and general location, and the nature of the facilities and assistance to be provided.
3. The agreement or agreements shall be negotiated as soon as possible on the initiative of the Security Council. They shall be concluded between the Security Council and Members or between the Security Council and groups of Members and shall be subject to ratification by the signatory states in accordance with their respective constitutional processes.

Article 44

When the Security Council has decided to use force it shall, before calling upon a Member not represented on it to provide armed forces in fulfilment of the obligations assumed under Article 43, invite that Member, if the Member so desires, to participate in the decisions of the Security Council concerning the employment of contingents of that Member's armed forces.

Article 45

In order to enable the United Nations to take urgent military measures, Members shall hold immediately available national air-force contingents for combined international enforcement action.

The strength and degree of readiness of these contingents and plans for their combined action shall be determined within the limits laid down in the special agreement or agreements referred to in Article 43, by the Security Council with the assistance of the Military Staff Committee.

Article 46

Plans for the application of armed force shall be made by the Security Council with the assistance of the Military Staff Committee.

Article 47

1. There shall be established a Military Staff Committee to advise and assist the Security Council on all questions relating to the Security Council's military requirements for the maintenance of international peace and security, the employment and command of forces placed at its disposal, the regulation of armaments, and possible disarmament.
2. The Military Staff Committee shall consist of the Chiefs of Staff of the permanent members of the Security Council or their representatives. Any Member of the United Nations not permanently represented on the Committee shall be invited by the Committee to be associated with it when the efficient discharge of the Committee's responsibilities requires the participation of that Member in its work.
3. The Military Staff Committee shall be responsible under the Security Council for the strategic direction of any armed forces placed at the disposal of the Security Council. Questions relating to the command of such forces shall be worked out subsequently.
4. The Military Staff Committee, with the authorization of the Security Council and after consultation with appropriate regional agencies, may establish regional sub-committees.

Article 48

1. The action required to carry out the decisions of the Security Council for the maintenance of international peace and security shall be taken by all the Members of the United Nations or by some of them, as the Security Council may determine.
2. Such decisions shall be carried out by the Members of the United Nations directly and through their action in the appropriate international agencies of which they are members.

Article 49

The Members of the United Nations shall join in affording mutual assistance in carrying out the measures decided upon by the Security Council.

Article 50

If preventive or enforcement measures against any state are taken by the Security Council, any other state, whether a Member of the United Nations or not, which finds itself confronted with special economic problems arising from the carrying out of those measures shall have the right to consult the Security Council with regard to a solution of those problems.

Article 51

Nothing in the present Charter shall impair the inherent right of individual or collective self-defence if an armed attack occurs against a Member of the United Nations, until the Security Council has taken measures necessary to maintain international peace and security. Measures taken by Members in the exercise of this right of self-defence shall be immediately reported to the Security Council and shall not in any way affect the authority and responsibility of the Security Council under the present Charter to take at any time such action as it deems necessary in order to maintain or restore international peace and security.

CHAPTER VIII: REGIONAL ARRANGEMENTS

Article 52
1. Nothing in the present Charter precludes the existence of regional arrangements or agencies for dealing with such matters relating to the maintenance of international peace and security as are appropriate for regional action provided that such arrangements or agencies and their activities are consistent with the Purposes and Principles of the United Nations.
2. The Members of the United Nations entering into such arrangements or constituting such agencies shall make every effort to achieve pacific settlement of local disputes through such regional arrangements or by such regional agencies before referring them to the Security Council.
3. The Security Council shall encourage the development of pacific settlement of local disputes through such regional arrangements or by such regional agencies either on the initiative of the states concerned or by reference from the Security Council.
4. This Article in no way impairs the application of Articles 34 and 35.

Article 53
1. The Security Council shall, where appropriate, utilize such regional arrangements or agencies for enforcement action under its authority. But no enforcement action shall be taken under regional arrangements or by regional agencies without the authorization of the Security Council, with the exception of measures against any enemy state, as defined in paragraph 2 of this Article, provided for pursuant to Article 107 or in regional arrangements directed against renewal of aggressive policy on the part of any such state, until such time as the Organization may, on request of the Governments concerned, be charged with the responsibility for preventing further aggression by such a state.

2. The term enemy state as used in paragraph 1 of this Article applies to any state which during the Second World War has been an enemy of any signatory of the present Charter.

Article 54

The Security Council shall at all times be kept fully informed of activities undertaken or in contemplation under regional arrangements or by regional agencies for the maintenance of international peace and security.

CHAPTER IX: INTERNATIONAL ECONOMIC AND SOCIAL CO-OPERATION

Article 55

With a view to the creation of conditions of stability and well-being which are necessary for peaceful and friendly relations among nations based on respect for the principle of equal rights and self-determination of peoples, the United Nations shall promote:

  a. higher standards of living, full employment, and conditions of economic and social progress and development;
  b. solutions of international economic, social, health, and related problems; and international cultural and educational cooperation; and
  c. universal respect for, and observance of, human rights and fundamental freedoms for all without distinction as to race, sex, language, or religion.

Article 56

All Members pledge themselves to take joint and separate action in co-operation with the Organization for the achievement of the purposes set forth in Article 55.

Article 57

1. The various specialized agencies, established by intergovernmental agreement and having wide international responsibilities, as defined in their basic instruments, in economic, social, cultural, educational, health, and related fields, shall be brought into relationship with the United Nations in accordance with the provisions of Article 63.
2. Such agencies thus brought into relationship with the United Nations are hereinafter referred to as specialized agencies.

Article 58

The Organization shall make recommendations for the co-ordination of the policies and activities of the specialized agencies.

Article 59

The Organization shall, where appropriate, initiate negotiations among the states concerned for the creation of any new specialized agencies required for the accomplishment of the purposes set forth in Article 55.

Article 60

Responsibility for the discharge of the functions of the Organization set forth in this Chapter shall be vested in the General Assembly and, under the authority of the General Assembly, in the Economic and Social Council, which shall have for this purpose the powers set forth in Chapter X.

CHAPTER X: THE ECONOMIC AND SOCIAL COUNCIL

COMPOSITION

Article 61

1. The Economic and Social Council shall consist of fifty-

four Members of the United Nations elected by the General Assembly.

2. Subject to the provisions of paragraph 3, eighteen members of the Economic and Social Council shall be elected each year for a term of three years. A retiring member shall be eligible for immediate re-election.

3. At the first election after the increase in the membership of the Economic and Social Council from twenty-seven to fifty-four members, in addition to the members elected in place of the nine members whose term of office expires at the end of that year, twenty-seven additional members shall be elected. Of these twenty-seven additional members, the term of office of nine members so elected shall expire at the end of one year, and of nine other members at the end of two years, in accordance with arrangements made by the General Assembly.

4. Each member of the Economic and Social Council shall have one representative.

FUNCTIONS and POWERS

Article 62

1. The Economic and Social Council may make or initiate studies and reports with respect to international economic, social, cultural, educational, health, and related matters and may make recommendations with respect to any such matters to the General Assembly to the Members of the United Nations, and to the specialized agencies concerned.

2. It may make recommendations for the purpose of promoting respect for, and observance of, human rights and fundamental freedoms for all.

3. It may prepare draft conventions for submission to the General Assembly, with respect to matters falling within its competence.

4. It may call, in accordance with the rules prescribed by the United Nations, international conferences on matters falling

within its competence.

Article 63

1. The Economic and Social Council may enter into agreements
   with any of the agencies referred to in Article 57, defining the
   terms on which the agency concerned shall be brought into
   relationship with the United Nations. Such agreements shall be
   subject to approval by the General Assembly.
2. It may co-ordinate the activities of the specialized agencies
   through consultation with and recommendations to such
   agencies and through recommendations to the General
   Assembly and to the Members of the United Nations.

Article 64

1. The Economic and Social Council may take appropriate
   steps to obtain regular reports from the specialized agencies.
   It may make arrangements with the Members of the United
   Nations and with the specialized agencies to obtain reports on
   the steps taken to give effect to its own recommendations and
   to recommendations on matters falling within its competence
   made by the General Assembly.
2. It may communicate its observations on these reports to the
   General Assembly.

Article 65

The Economic and Social Council may furnish information to
the Security Council and shall assist the Security Council upon its
request.

Article 66

1. The Economic and Social Council shall perform such functions
   as fall within its competence in connection with the carrying
   out of the recommendations of the General Assembly.
2. It may, with the approval of the General Assembly, perform

services at the request of Members of the United Nations and at the request of specialized agencies.

3. It shall perform such other functions as are specified elsewhere in the present Charter or as may be assigned to it by the General Assembly.

VOTING

Article 67

1. Each member of the Economic and Social Council shall have one vote.
2. Decisions of the Economic and Social Council shall be made by a majority of the members present and voting.

PROCEDURE

Article 68

The Economic and Social Council shall set up commissions in economic and social fields and for the promotion of human rights, and such other commissions as may be required for the performance of its functions.

Article 69

The Economic and Social Council shall invite any Member of the United Nations to participate, without vote, in its deliberations on any matter of particular concern to that Member.

Article 70

The Economic and Social Council may make arrangements for representatives of the specialized agencies to participate, without vote, in its deliberations and in those of the commissions established by it, and for its representatives to participate in the deliberations of the specialized agencies.

Article 71

The Economic and Social Council may make suitable arrangements for consultation with non-governmental organizations which are concerned with matters within its competence. Such arrangements may be made with international organizations and, where appropriate, with national organizations after consultation with the Member of the United Nations concerned.

Article 72

1. The Economic and Social Council shall adopt its own rules of procedure, including the method of selecting its President.
2. The Economic and Social Council shall meet as required in accordance with its rules, which shall include provision for the convening of meetings on the request of a majority of its members.

CHAPTER XI: DECLARATION REGARDING NON-SELF-GOVERNING TERRITORIES

Article 73

Members of the United Nations which have or assume responsibilities for the administration of territories whose peoples have not yet attained a full measure of self-government recognize the principle that the interests of the inhabitants of these territories are paramount, and accept as a sacred trust the obligation to promote to the utmost, within the system of international peace and security established by the present Charter, the well-being of the inhabitants of these territories, and, to this end:

   a. to ensure, with due respect for the culture of the peoples concerned, their political, economic, social, and educational advancement, their just treatment, and their protection against abuses;

b. to develop self-government, to take due account of the political aspirations of the peoples, and to assist them in the progressive development of their free political institutions, according to the particular circumstances of each territory and its peoples and their varying stages of advancement;
c. to further international peace and security;
d. to promote constructive measures of development, to encourage research, and to co-operate with one another and, when and where appropriate, with specialized international bodies with a view to the practical achievement of the social, economic, and scientific purposes set forth in this Article; and
e. to transmit regularly to the Secretary-General for information purposes, subject to such limitation as security and constitutional considerations may require, statistical and other information of a technical nature relating to economic, social, and educational conditions in the territories for which they are respectively responsible other than those territories to which Chapters XII and XIII apply.

Article 74

Members of the United Nations also agree that their policy in respect of the territories to which this Chapter applies, no less than in respect of their metropolitan areas, must be based on the general principle of good-neighbourliness, due account being taken of the interests and well-being of the rest of the world, in social, economic, and commercial matters.

CHAPTER XII: INTERNATIONAL TRUSTEESHIP SYSTEM

Article 75
The United Nations shall establish under its authority an international trusteeship system for the administration and supervision of such territories as may be placed thereunder by subsequent individual agreements. These territories are hereinafter referred to as trust territories.

Article 76
The basic objectives of the trusteeship system, in accordance with the Purposes of the United Nations laid down in Article 1 of the present Charter, shall be:

a. to further international peace and security;
b. to promote the political, economic, social, and educational advancement of the inhabitants of the trust territories, and their progressive development towards self-government or independence as may be appropriate to the particular circumstances of each territory and its peoples and the freely expressed wishes of the peoples concerned, and as may be provided by the terms of each trusteeship agreement;
c. to encourage respect for human rights and for fundamental freedoms for all without distinction as to race, sex, language, or religion, and to encourage recognition of the interdependence of the peoples of the world; and
d. to ensure equal treatment in social, economic, and commercial matters for all Members of the United Nations and their nationals, and also equal treatment for the latter in the administration of justice, without prejudice to the attainment of the foregoing objectives and subject to the provisions of Article 80.

Article 77

1. The trusteeship system shall apply to such territories in the following categories as may be placed thereunder by means of trusteeship agreements:
   a. territories now held under mandate;
   b. territories which may be detached from enemy states as a result of the Second World War; and
   c. territories voluntarily placed under the system by states responsible for their administration.

2. It will be a matter for subsequent agreement as to which territories in the foregoing categories will be brought under the trusteeship system and upon what terms.

Article 78

The trusteeship system shall not apply to territories which have become Members of the United Nations, relationship among which shall be based on respect for the principle of sovereign equality.

Article 79

The terms of trusteeship for each territory to be placed under the trusteeship system, including any alteration or amendment, shall be agreed upon by the states directly concerned, including the mandatory power in the case of territories held under mandate by a Member of the United Nations, and shall be approved as provided for in Articles 83 and 85.

Article 80

1. Except as may be agreed upon in individual trusteeship agreements, made under Articles 77, 79, and 81, placing each territory under the trusteeship system, and until such agreements have been concluded, nothing in this Chapter shall be construed in or of itself to alter in any manner the rights whatsoever of any states or any peoples or the terms of existing

international instruments to which Members of the United
Nations may respectively be parties.

2. Paragraph 1 of this Article shall not be interpreted as giving
    grounds for delay or postponement of the negotiation and
    conclusion of agreements for placing mandated and other
    territories under the trusteeship system as provided for in
    Article 77.

Article 81

The trusteeship agreement shall in each case include the terms
under which the trust territory will be administered and designate
the authority which will exercise the administration of the trust
territory. Such authority, hereinafter called the administering
authority, may be one or more states or the Organization itself.

Article 82

There may be designated, in any trusteeship agreement, a strategic
area or areas which may include part or all of the trust territory
to which the agreement applies, without prejudice to any special
agreement or agreements made under Article 43.

Article 83

1. All functions of the United Nations relating to strategic areas,
    including the approval of the terms of the trusteeship agreements
    and of their alteration or amendment shall be exercised by the
    Security Council.
2. The basic objectives set forth in Article 76 shall be applicable to
    the people of each strategic area.
3. The Security Council shall, subject to the provisions of the
    trusteeship agreements and without prejudice to security
    considerations, avail itself of the assistance of the Trusteeship
    Council to perform those functions of the United Nations under
    the trusteeship system relating to political, economic, social,
    and educational matters in the strategic areas.

Article 84

It shall be the duty of the administering authority to ensure that the trust territory shall play its part in the maintenance of international peace and security. To this end the administering authority may make use of volunteer forces, facilities, and assistance from the trust territory in carrying out the obligations towards the Security Council undertaken in this regard by the administering authority, as well as for local defence and the maintenance of law and order within the trust territory.

Article 85

1. The functions of the United Nations with regard to trusteeship agreements for all areas not designated as strategic, including the approval of the terms of the trusteeship agreements and of their alteration or amendment, shall be exercised by the General Assembly.
2. The Trusteeship Council, operating under the authority of the General Assembly shall assist the General Assembly in carrying out these functions.

CHAPTER XIII: THE TRUSTEESHIP COUNCIL

COMPOSITION

Article 86

1. The Trusteeship Council shall consist of the following Members of the United Nations:
    a. those Members administering trust territories;
    b. such of those Members mentioned by name in Article 23 as are not administering trust territories; and
    c. as many other Members elected for three-year terms by the General Assembly as may be necessary to ensure that the total number of members of the Trusteeship Council

is equally divided between those Members of the United Nations which administer trust territories and those which do not.

2. Each member of the Trusteeship Council shall designate one specially qualified person to represent it therein.

FUNCTIONS and POWERS

Article 87
The General Assembly and, under its authority, the Trusteeship Council, in carrying out their functions, may:
   a. consider reports submitted by the administering authority;
   b. accept petitions and examine them in consultation with the administering authority;
   c. provide for periodic visits to the respective trust territories at times agreed upon with the administering authority; and
   d. take these and other actions in conformity with the terms of the trusteeship agreements.

Article 88
The Trusteeship Council shall formulate a questionnaire on the political, economic, social, and educational advancement of the inhabitants of each trust territory, and the administering authority for each trust territory within the competence of the General Assembly shall make an annual report to the General Assembly upon the basis of such questionnaire.

VOTING

Article 89
1. Each member of the Trusteeship Council shall have one vote.
2. Decisions of the Trusteeship Council shall be made by a majority of the members present and voting.

PROCEDURE

Article 90
1. The Trusteeship Council shall adopt its own rules of procedure, including the method of selecting its President.
2. The Trusteeship Council shall meet as required in accordance with its rules, which shall include provision for the convening of meetings on the request of a majority of its members.

Article 91
The Trusteeship Council shall, when appropriate, avail itself of the assistance of the Economic and Social Council and of the specialized agencies in regard to matters with which they are respectively concerned.

CHAPTER XIV: THE INTERNATIONAL COURT OF JUSTICE

Article 92
The International Court of Justice shall be the principal judicial organ of the United Nations. It shall function in accordance with the annexed Statute, which is based upon the Statute of the Permanent Court of International Justice and forms an integral part of the present Charter.

Article 93
1. All Members of the United Nations are ipso facto parties to the Statute of the International Court of Justice.
2. A state which is not a Member of the United Nations may become a party to the Statute of the International Court of Justice on conditions to be determined in each case by the General Assembly upon the recommendation of the Security Council.

Article 94

1. Each Member of the United Nations undertakes to comply with the decision of the International Court of Justice in any case to which it is a party.
2. If any party to a case fails to perform the obligations incumbent upon it under a judgment rendered by the Court, the other party may have recourse to the Security Council, which may, if it deems necessary, make recommendations or decide upon measures to be taken to give effect to the judgment.

Article 95

Nothing in the present Charter shall prevent Members of the United Nations from entrusting the solution of their differences to other tribunals by virtue of agreements already in existence or which may be concluded in the future.

Article 96

a. The General Assembly or the Security Council may request the International Court of Justice to give an advisory opinion on any legal question.
b. Other organs of the United Nations and specialized agencies, which may at any time be so authorized by the General Assembly, may also request advisory opinions of the Court on legal questions arising within the scope of their activities.

CHAPTER XV: THE SECRETARIAT

Article 97

The Secretariat shall comprise a Secretary-General and such staff as the Organization may require. The Secretary-General shall be appointed by the General Assembly upon the recommendation of the Security Council. He shall be the chief administrative officer of the Organization.

Article 98

The Secretary-General shall act in that capacity in all meetings of the General Assembly, of the Security Council, of the Economic and Social Council, and of the Trusteeship Council, and shall perform such other functions as are entrusted to him by these organs. The Secretary-General shall make an annual report to the General Assembly on the work of the Organization.

Article 99

The Secretary-General may bring to the attention of the Security Council any matter which in his opinion may threaten the maintenance of international peace and security.

Article 100

1. In the performance of their duties the Secretary-General and the staff shall not seek or receive instructions from any government or from any other authority external to the Organization. They shall refrain from any action which might reflect on their position as international officials responsible only to the Organization.
2. Each Member of the United Nations undertakes to respect the exclusively international character of the responsibilities of the Secretary-General and the staff and not to seek to influence them in the discharge of their responsibilities.

Article 101

1. The staff shall be appointed by the Secretary-General under regulations established by the General Assembly.
2. Appropriate staffs shall be permanently assigned to the Economic and Social Council, the Trusteeship Council, and, as required, to other organs of the United Nations. These staffs shall form a part of the Secretariat.
3. The paramount consideration in the employment of the staff and in the determination of the conditions of service shall be

the necessity of securing the highest standards of efficiency, competence, and integrity. Due regard shall be paid to the importance of recruiting the staff on as wide a geographical basis as possible.

CHAPTER XVI: MISCELLANEOUS PROVISIONS

Article 102
1. Every treaty and every international agreement entered into by any Member of the United Nations after the present Charter comes into force shall as soon as possible be registered with the Secretariat and published by it.
2. No party to any such treaty or international agreement which has not been registered in accordance with the provisions of paragraph 1 of this Article may invoke that treaty or agreement before any organ of the United Nations.

Article 103
In the event of a conflict between the obligations of the Members of the United Nations under the present Charter and their obligations under any other international agreement, their obligations under the present Charter shall prevail.

Article 104
The Organization shall enjoy in the territory of each of its Members such legal capacity as may be necessary for the exercise of its functions and the fulfilment of its purposes.

Article 105
1. The Organization shall enjoy in the territory of each of its Members such privileges and immunities as are necessary for the fulfilment of its purposes.
2. Representatives of the Members of the United Nations and

officials of the Organization shall similarly enjoy such privileges and immunities as are necessary for the independent exercise of their functions in connexion with the Organization.

3. The General Assembly may make recommendations with a view to determining the details of the application of paragraphs 1 and 2 of this Article or may propose conventions to the Members of the United Nations for this purpose.

CHAPTER XVII: TRANSITIONAL SECURITY ARRANGEMENTS

Article 106

Pending the coming into force of such special agreements referred to in Article 43 as in the opinion of the Security Council enable it to begin the exercise of its responsibilities under Article 42, the parties to the Four-Nation Declaration, signed at Moscow, 30 October 1943, and France, shall, in accordance with the provisions of paragraph 5 of that Declaration, consult with one another and as occasion requires with other Members of the United Nations with a view to such joint action on behalf of the Organization as may be necessary for the purpose of maintaining international peace and security.

Article 107

Nothing in the present Charter shall invalidate or preclude action, in relation to any state which during the Second World War has been an enemy of any signatory to the present Charter, taken or authorized as a result of that war by the Governments having responsibility for such action.

CHAPTER XVIII: AMENDMENTS

Article 108
Amendments to the present Charter shall come into force for all Members of the United Nations when they have been adopted by a vote of two thirds of the members of the General Assembly and ratified in accordance with their respective constitutional processes by two thirds of the Members of the United Nations, including all the permanent members of the Security Council.

Article 109
1. A General Conference of the Members of the United Nations for the purpose of reviewing the present Charter may be held at a date and place to be fixed by a two-thirds vote of the members of the General Assembly and by a vote of any nine members of the Security Council. Each Member of the United Nations shall have one vote in the conference.
2. Any alteration of the present Charter recommended by a two-thirds vote of the conference shall take effect when ratified in accordance with their respective constitutional processes by two thirds of the Members of the United Nations including all the permanent members of the Security Council.
3. If such a conference has not been held before the tenth annual session of the General Assembly following the coming into force of the present Charter, the proposal to call such a conference shall be placed on the agenda of that session of the General Assembly, and the conference shall be held if so decided by a majority vote of the members of the General Assembly and by a vote of any seven members of the Security Council.

CHAPTER XIX: RATIFICATION AND SIGNATURE

Article 110

1. The present Charter shall be ratified by the signatory states in accordance with their respective constitutional processes.
2. The ratifications shall be deposited with the Government of the United States of America, which shall notify all the signatory states of each deposit as well as the Secretary-General of the Organization when he has been appointed.
3. The present Charter shall come into force upon the deposit of ratifications by the Republic of China, France, the Union of Soviet Socialist Republics, the United Kingdom of Great Britain and Northern Ireland, and the United States of America, and by a majority of the other signatory states. A protocol of the ratifications deposited shall thereupon be drawn up by the Government of the United States of America which shall communicate copies thereof to all the signatory states.
4. The states signatory to the present Charter which ratify it after it has come into force will become original Members of the United Nations on the date of the deposit of their respective ratifications.

Article 111

The present Charter, of which the Chinese, French, Russian, English, and Spanish texts are equally authentic, shall remain deposited in the archives of the Government of the United States of America. Duly certified copies thereof shall be transmitted by that Government to the Governments of the other signatory states.

IN FAITH WHEREOF the representatives of the Governments of the United Nations have signed the present Charter. DONE at the city of San Francisco the twenty-sixth day of June, one thousand nine hundred and forty-five.

Appendix 3

PROF. DR. (MULT.) KAMIL E. IDRIS CV

President
The International Court of Arbitration and Mediation (ICAM)

Former Director General
World Intellectual Property Organization (WIPO)

Former Secretary-General
International Union for the Protection of New Varieties of Plants (UPOV)

Former Member
United Nations International Law Commission (ILC)

Former President
World Arbitration and Mediation Court (WAMC)

Member
Permanent Court of Arbitration (PCA), The Hague

Professor of Law

Academic Distinctions
• Sudan School Certificate (Distinction)

- Bachelor of Arts, University of Cairo (Division I with Honours)
- LLB (Law), University of Khartoum (Honours)
- Diploma, Public Administration (Management Department), Institute of Public Administration, Khartoum (Top Division)
- Master in International Affairs, University of Ohio, USA (First Class Average)
- Doctorate (PhD) in International Law, Graduate Institute of International Studies, University of Geneva (Distinction)
- Doctorate Thesis: "Case study on the Treaty Establishing a Preferential Trade Area for Eastern and Southern African States

Academic Interests

Certificates
- International Economics, Graduate Institute of International Studies (Geneva)
- International History and Political Science, Graduate Institute of International Studies (Geneva)
- International Law of Development, Graduate Institute of International Studies (Geneva)
- The Law of International Waterways, Graduate Institute of International Studies (Geneva)
- International Law of Financing and Banking Systems, Graduate Institute of International Studies (Geneva)

Languages
- Arabic
- English
- French
- Spanish (good knowledge)

Teaching
- Lecturer in Philosophy and Jurisprudence, University of Cairo (1976-1977)

- Lecturer in Jurisprudence, Ohio University, USA (1978)
- External Examiner in International Law, Faculty of Law, University of Khartoum (1984)
- Lecturer in Intellectual Property Law, Faculty of Law, University of Khartoum (1986)
- Lecturer in several international, regional and national seminars, workshops and symposia
- Member, International Association for the Advancement of Teaching and Research in Intellectual Property Law (ATRIP)

Decorations
- Awarded the Scholars and Researchers State Gold Medal, presented by the President of the Republic of the Sudan (1983)
- Awarded the Scholars and Researchers Gold Medal, presented by the President of the Academy of Scientific Research and Technology of Egypt (1985)
- Awarded the decoration of the Commandeur de l'Ordre national du Lion, Senegal (1998)
- Awarded the Medal of the Bolshoi Theatre, presented by the Director of the Bolshoi Theatre, Russian Federation (1999)
- Awarded the Honorary Medal, presented by the Rector of the Moscow State Institute of International Relations, Russian Federation (1999)
- Awarded the Honorary Medal of The Gulf Cooperation Council (GCC), Saudi Arabia (1999)
- Awarded the Golden Plaque of the Town of Banská Bystrica, presented by the Mayor of Banská Bystrica, Slovakia (1999)
- Awarded the Golden Medal of Matej Bel University, presented by the Dean of the University, Banská Bystrica, Slovakia (1999)
- Awarded the Silver Jubilee Medal of the Eurasian Patent Organization (EAPO), presented by Mr. Viktor Blinnikov, President of the Eurasian Patent Office, Russian Federation (2000)
- Award of Distinguished Merit, presented by the Egyptian

Supreme Council for Science and Technology, Egypt (2000)
- Awarded a Plaque from the Syrian Inventors' Association, Syrian Arab Republic (2000)
- Awarded the Grand Cross of the Infante D. Enrique, Portugal (2001)
- Awarded a Medal from the People's Assembly of Egypt, Egypt (2001)
- Awarded a Medal from the Constitutional Court of Romania, Romania (2001)
- Awarded a Medal from the Parliament of Romania, Romania (2001)
- Awarded the Golden Medal Dolores del Río al Mérito internacional en favor de los derechos de los artistas intérpretes from the National Association of Interpreters (ANDI), Mexico (2001)
- Awarded the Golden Medal from The State Agency on Industrial Property Protection, Republic of Moldova (2001)
- Awarded the decoration of the Commandeur de l'Ordre du Mérite national, Côte d'Ivoire (2002)
- Awarded the Maria Sklodowska-Curie Medal from the Association of Polish Inventors and Rationalizers, Poland (2002)
- Awarded the decoration of The Order of the Two Niles, First Class, from the President of the Republic of Sudan, Sudan (2002)
- Kamil Idris Library, University of Juba, Sudan (2002)
- Kamil Idris Conference Hall, Intellectual Property Court, The Judiciary, Sudan (2002)
- Awarded the Dank Medal (medal of glory), from the President of the Kyrgyz Republic, Kyrgyzstan (2003)
- Award from the University of National and World Economy, Bulgaria (2003)
- "Venice Award for Intellectual Property", presented by the Mayor of Venice (2004)
- Awarded the Medal of Oman, presented by His Royal Highness Fahid Bin Mahmud Al-Said, Deputy Prime Minister of the

Council of Ministers, Oman (2004)
- Awarded the decoration of the Aztec Eagle, presented by Ambassador Luis Alfonso de Alba (Permanent Representative of Mexico to International Organizations in Geneva) on behalf of Presidente of Mexico Vicente Fox, (2005)
- Kamil Idris Building, Regional Training Center, African Regional Intellectual Property Organization (ARIPO), Harare, Zimbabwe (2006)
- Awarded a Medal commemorating the 60 years of the United Nations, Bulgaria (2006)
- Awarded a Medal commemorating the 60 years of the Independence of Jordan, Jordan (2006)
- Award of Distinguished Leadership presented by the International Publishers'Association (IPA) and the Arab Publishers Association, Egypt (2007)
- Awarded a Medal on the occasion of the Fujairah International Monodrama Festival, Fujairah,United Arab Emirates (2007)
- Awarded a Medal on the occasion of the Intellectual Property Day presented by The Regional Institute for Intellectual Property of the Faculty of Law, University of Helwan, Egypt (2008)
- Awarded The Distinguished Medal of Cultural Innovation, Sudan (2008)
- Awarded The Family Club Decoration, Sudan (2008)
- Awarded The World Intellectual Property Organization (WIPO) Medal, Geneva, Switzerland(2008)
- Awarded The International Union Of The Protection Of New Varieties Of Plants (UPOV)
- Medal, Geneva, Switzerland (2008)
- Awarded The Distinguished Medal Of The Sudanese Centre Of Intellectual Property, Khartoum, Sudan (2009)
- Awarded The Medal Of Kenana sugar Company, Khartoum , Sudan (2009)
- Awarded The Decoration Of Loyalty And Gratitude Of

Omdurman National Broadcasting Station, Sudan (2010)
- Awarded The decoration (WISHAH) of the Syrian revolution (2013)
- Awarded The decoration (WISHAH) of Rashid Diab cultural center, Khartoum , Sudan (2013)
- Awarded The Medal of Distinction by the International Association of Muslim
- Lawyers (2014)

Honorary Degrees
- 1999 Honorary Professor of Law, Peking University, China
- 1999 Doctor Honoris Causa, The Doctor's Council of the State University of Moldova, Republic of Moldova
- 1999 Doctor Honoris Causa, Franklin Pierce Law Center (Concord, New Hampshire), United States of America
- 1999 Doctor Honoris Causa, Fudan University (Shanghai), China
- 2000 Doctor Honoris Causa, University of National and World Economy (Sofia), Bulgaria
- 2001 Doctor Honoris Causa, University of Bucharest, Romania
- 2001 Doctor Honoris Causa, Hannam University (Daejeon), Republic of Korea
- 2001 Doctor Honoris Causa, Mongolian University of Science and Technology (Ulaanbaatar), Mongolia
- 2001 Doctor Honoris Causa, Matej Bel University (Banská Bystrica), Slovakia
- 2002 Doctor Honoris Causa, National Technical University of Ukraine "Kyiv Polytechnic Institute" (Kyiv), Ukraine
- 2003 Doctor Honoris Causa, Al Eman Al Mahdi University (White Nile State), Sudan
- 2005 Degree of Doctor of Letters (Honoris Causa), Indira Gandhi National Open University (IGNOU), India
- 2005 Doctor Honoris Causa, Latvian Academy of Sciences, Latvia

- 2006 Doctor Honoris Causa, University of Azerbaijan, Azerbaijan
- 2007 Doctor Honoris Causa, University of Al-Gezira, Sudan
- 2007 Doctor of International Law and Honorary Professor, Belarussian State University, Belarus
- 2007 Doctor Honoris Causa, University of Khartoum, Sudan
- 2007 Doctor Honoris Causa, Ss. Cyril and Methodius University (Skopje), The Former Yugoslav Republic of Macedonia
- 2008 Doctor Honoris Causa, Kyrgyz State University of Construction, Transport and Architecture (Bishkek), Kyrgystan
- 2008 Certificate of Appreciation, Ahlia University, Khartoum, Sudan

Experience

Professional

- Part-time Journalist, El-Ayam and El-Sahafa (Sudanese) newspapers (1971-1979)
- Lecturer, University of Cairo (1976)
- Assistant Director, Arab Department, Ministry of Foreign Affairs, Khartoum (1977)
- Assistant Director, Research Department, Ministry of Foreign Affairs, Khartoum (January-June 1978)
- Deputy Director, Legal Department, Ministry of Foreign Affairs, Khartoum (July-December 1978)
- Member of Sudan Permanent Mission to the United Nations Office, Geneva (1979-1982)
- Vice-Consul of Sudan in Switzerland (1979-1982)
- Legal Adviser of Sudan Permanent Mission to the United Nations Office, Geneva (1979-1982)
- Senior Program Officer, Development Cooperation and External Relations Bureau for Africa, World Intellectual Property Organization (WIPO), (1982-1985)
- Director, Development Cooperation and External Relations

Bureau for Arab and Central and Eastern European Countries, WIPO (1985-1994)
- Ambassador, Ministry of Foreign Affairs, Sudan (current status at national level)
- Deputy Director General, WIPO (1994-1997)
- Director General, WIPO, since 1997
- Secretary-General, International Union for the Protection of Plant Varieties (UPOV), since 1997

Special
- Member of The Academic Council, University of Khartoum (Sudan, April 2007)
- Member, Board of Trustees, Nile Valley University (Egypt, June 2000)
- Member, United Nations International Law Commission (ILC) (2000-2001)
- Member, Advisory Council on Intellectual Property (ACIP), Franklin Pierce Law Center (Concord, New Hampshire, 1999)
- Member, United Nations International Law Commission (ILC) (1992-1996)
- Vice-Chairman of the International Law Commission (ILC) at its 45th session (1993)
- Representative of the ILC in the 35th session of the Asian-African Legal Consultative Committee (AALCC) (Manila, March 1996)
- Member, Working Group of the ILC on the drafting of the Statute of the International Criminal Court
- Member, Drafting Committee of the ILC
- Legal expert in a number of Ministerial Committees between Sudan and other countries
- Member of the Legal Experts Committee of the Organization of African Unity (OAU), which formulated several regional conventions
- Legal adviser in the Ministerial Councils and the Summit

Conferences of the OAU (Khartoum, July 1978) (Monrovia, July 1979)

- Participant in several meetings and international conferences of WHO, ILO, ITU, WIPO, Red Cross and the Executive Committee of the High Commissioner for Refugees
- Member of Special Committees established for fundraising for refugees in Africa
- Rapporteur of the Third Committee (Marine Scientific Research) of the summary Ninth session of the Third UN Conference on the Law of the Sea (Geneva, 1980)
- Head of Sudan Delegation to the OAU Preparatory Meeting on the Draft Code of Conduct on Transfer of Technology (Addis Ababa, March 1981)
- Spokesman of the African Group and the Group of 77 on all issues pertaining to Transfer of Technology, Energy, Restrictive Business Practices and Technical Co-operation among Developing Countries at the twenty-second and twenty-third sessions of the Trade and Development Board (Geneva, February and September 1981
- Head of Sudan Delegation and Spokesman of the African Group and Coordinator of the Group of 77 at the fourth session of the UN Conference on the Code of Conduct on Transfer of Technology (Geneva, March-April 1981)
- Spokesman of the Group of 77 on Chapter 9 (Applicable Law and Settlement of Disputes) at the UN Conference on the International Code of Conduct on Transfer of Technology (Geneva, March-April 1981)
- Head of Sudan Delegation and Chairman of the Workshop on Legal Policies on Technology Transfer (Kuwait, September 1981)
- Chairman of the African Group and the Group of 77 at the first session of the Intergovernmental Group of Experts on Restrictive Business Practices (Geneva, November 1981)
- Chairman of the Permanent Group of 15 on Transfer and

Development of Technology, within the United Nations Conference on Trade and Development (UNCTAD) (Geneva, 1980-1983)

- Spokesman of the African Group and the Group of 77 at the meeting on the Economic, Commercial and Developmental Aspects of the Industrial Property System (Geneva, February 1982)
- Coordinator of the African Group and the Group of 77 at the first, second and third sessions of the Interim Committee on the International Code of Conduct on Transfer of Technology (Geneva, March, May, September-October 1982)
- Coordinator of the African Group and the Group of 77 at the Meeting of Governmental Experts on the Transfer, Application and Development of Technology in the Capital Goods and Industrial Machinery Sectors (Geneva, July 1982)
- Coordinator and spokesman of the African Group and the Group of 77 at the Intergovernmental Group of Experts on the Feasibility of Measuring Human Resource Flows on Reverse Transfer of Technology (Brain-Drain) (Geneva, August-September 1982)
- Coordinator of developing countries on the drafting of the resolution concerning the mandate of the Office of the United Nations High Commissioner for Refugees, during the thirty-third session of the Executive Committee of the UNHCR (Geneva, October 1982)
- Coordinator and spokesman of the African Group and the Group of 77 at the Meeting of Governmental Experts on the Transfer, Application and Development of Technology in the Energy Sector (Geneva, October-November 1982)
- Coordinator and spokesman of the African Group and the Group of 77 at the fourth session of the Committee on Transfer of Technology (Geneva, November-December 1982)
- Member, Board of Patrons, IP Management Resource (On-line version of Intellectual Property/Innovation Management

Handbook), 2007
- Co-President, Foreign Relations Committee, Ministry of Culture (Sudan, 2011)
- President, Sudan Foundation for the defense of Syrian people (2012-2013)
- Vice-President, Sudan Foundation for the defense of Rights and Freedom s (2012-2013)
- Member, Sudan Foundation for Reconciliation and Religious co-existence (2012-2013)
- Judicial Experience and Professional Membership of Associations
- Member of the United Nations International Law Commission (ILC) (1992-1996) and (2000-2001)
- Member and Chairman of several legal experts committees established within the OAU
- Professor of Public International Law, University of Khartoum, Sudan
- Member of the Sudan Bar Association (Khartoum)
- Member of the African Jurists Association (Dakar and Paris)
- Alternate Chair, Council of Foreign Relations, Ministry of Culture, Sudan
- Registered Advocate and Commissioner for Oaths in the Republic of Sudan
- Vice President, Sudan Organisation for the Protection of Fundamental Rights and Freedoms
- Member, Sudan High Level Committee on Judicial Reform

Projects and Documents
- Formulated and negotiated, on behalf of WIPO, numerous projects relating to development cooperation in the field of intellectual property
- Organized, on behalf of WIPO, various seminars and workshops and presented several lectures
- Drafted various documents on developmental aspects of

intellectual property
- Supervised and managed the administrative and substantive aspects of projects executed worldwide

Conferences, Seminars, Courses and Symposia
- Represented Sudan in numerous international and regional conferences; participated in many seminars, symposia, discussion groups, and addressed graduate students on various international academic disciplines
- Represented WIPO, in various international meetings, seminars and symposia
- Represented WIPO on several UNDP Policy and Operations Programmes
- Undertook a study tour at the Max Planck Institute (Munich) in the field of teaching of intellectual property law (1986)

Publications
- Euro-Arab Dialogue, June 1977
- State Responsibility in International Law, September 1977
- The Theory of Human Action, September 1977
- The Philosophy of "Haddith" and "Sunna" in Islamic Law, January 1978
- The Doctrine of Jurisdiction in International Law, December 1978
- American Embassy in Tehran Case, March 1979
- The Legal Regime of the Nile, December 1980
- Issues pertaining to Transfer and Development of Technology in Sudan, May 1981
- China and the Powers in the 19th Century, May 1981
- Legal Dimensions of the Economic Cooperation among Developing Countries, June 1981
- The Common Fund for Commodities, June 1981
- General Aspects of Transfer of Technology at the National and International Levels, November 1981

- Preferential Trading Arrangements among Developing Countries, February 1982
- North-South Insurance Relations: The Unequal Exchange, December 1984
- The Law of Non-Navigational Uses of International Water Courses; the International Law Commission's draft articles: An overview, November 1995
- The Theory of Source and Target in Child Psychology, January 1996
- A Better United Nations for the New Millennium, January 2000
- Intellectual Property – A Power Tool for Economic Growth, 2003
- Sudan, The Year 2020: Lessons and Visions, 2004
- The Intellectual Property-Conscious Nations: Mapping the Path from Developing to Developed, 2006
- Sudan 2020, (2008)
- Sudan: From Least-Developed to Fast Developing, 2008
- Arbitration: A Vision for the Enforcement of Justice, 2009
- Arbitration: Critical Review Of Sudan Legislation On Arbitration, 2009
- Sudan 2025: The Correction of the Path and the Dream of the Future, 2015
- Seven Deaths on the Nile, 2015
- Sudan's Path to the Future: A realistic dream for 2025, 2016
- A Memoir: Odyssey on the Nile, 2017

Articles
- A number of articles on law, economics, jurisprudence and aesthetics published in various newspapers and periodicals
- Russia's Invasion of Crimea: Is it a violation of International Law? Two mistakes will not make a right. Article published by The Hague Center for Law and Arbitration (HCLA) April, 2014
- Law Reform in Sudan: March, 2015

Photo licences

All images in this publication are listed as 'In the Public Domain' other than those listed below:

- Adolf Hitler: © *Mihailo1997*
  – *Creative Commons Attribution-Share Alike 4.0 International*
- Nelson Mandela: © *South Africa The Good News*
  – *Creative Commons Attribution 2.0 Generic*
- Tarek El-Tayeb Mohamed Bouazizi: © *Chris Belsten*
  – *Attribution-ShareAlike 2.0 Generic*
- Arab Spring, photo 1: © *Jonathan Rashad*
  – *Creative Commons Attribution 2.0 Generic*
- Arab Spring, photo 2: © *Ramy Raoof*
  – *Creative Commons Attribution 2.0 Generic*
- Kashmir conflict: © *Jrapczak*
  – *Creative Commons Attribution-Share Alike 3.0 Unported*
- North Korea: © Stefan Krasowski
  – *Attribution 2.0 Generic*
- The Israeli / Palestinian conflict, photo 1: © *Israel Defense Forces*
  – *Creative Commons Attribution-Share Alike 2.0 Generic*
- The Israeli / Palestinian conflict, photo 2: © *gloucester2gaza*
  – *Creative Commons Attribution-Share Alike 2.0 Generic*

Index

A

Afghanistan, 16, 113
Africa, 6, 12, 36, 59, 99, 110, 116, 165, 167, 172
Al Qaeda, 12
Arab, 12, 16, 35-37, 40, 42, 51-52, 55, 59-63, 110, 113, 115, 161, 163, 165, 172
Assad, 40-44, 50
Austria, 8, 38, 77, 86, 88, 91, 93-94, 106
Austria-Hungary, 10, 86-87, 89-90, 93-94, 96, 98

C

China, 23, 28, 48, 50, 67, 72-73, 79, 82-83, 99, 111, 113-114, 130, 158, 164, 170
Churchill, 20, 69-70, 96-97, 106-107, 111, 119
Crimea, 32, 39, 66, 76, 171
Cuba, 27

E

Egypt, 36-37, 57, 59-60, 62, 67, 109, 115, 161-163, 166
EU, 34, 38-39, 67-69, 72, 74, 76-79, 110, 116
Europe, 7, 24, 33-34, 37-39, 43, 50, 53, 55, 69, 71, 76, 78-79, 81, 83, 90-92, 94, 97-100

F

Ferdinand, 10, 86-88, 93
First World War, 24-25, 53, 66, 71, 85-86, 98, 104, 108
France, 23, 37-38, 50, 52, 66, 68, 73, 77, 90-93, 95-96, 99, 102, 130, 156, 158

U

UK, 7, 23, 26, 37, 39, 50, 52, 65-66, 68-69, 110, 118

Ukraine, 32-34, 43, 66, 73, 83-84, 164

UN, 19, 31-32, 36, 46, 49, 52-53, 56, 60-63, 70, 72-75, 77-78, 121, 167

US, 1-2, 4-17, 20, 22-25, 27, 31, 33-34, 39, 41-44, 50, 52, 60-63, 65-67, 69-70, 72-73, 76, 84, 108-109, 111

X

Xi Jinping, 82-83, 114

Y

Yemen, 15, 36, 50, 52-53